» *V I S I O N I* «

» *18* «

DĪVĀN-I SHAMS-I TABRĪZ

FORTY-EIGHT GHAZALS

JALĀL AD-DĪN RŪMĪ

Dīvān-i Shams-i Tabrīz

FORTY-EIGHT GHAZALS

EDITED AND TRANSLATED BY
IRAJ ANVAR

FOREWORD BY PETER CHELKOWSKI

INTRODUCTION BY
MOḤAMMAD ʿALĪ MOVAHED

semar

Rūmī, Jalāl ad-dīn,
Dīvān-i Shams-i Tabrīz. Forty-eight Ghazals.
Jalāl ad-dīn Rūmī;
Roma: Semar 2002, 180 pp. - 17 cm;
(Semar: Visioni 18).

ISBN 88-7778-080-0

Fisrt edition March 2002

Cover Zoomorphic Basmalah, Irān, eighteenth century.
Frontispiece Portrait of Rūmī, and a
calligraphic inscription *[Ya Hazrat Mowlānā,
Praise be to Our Master, may God keep his secret]*
in *Nasta'līq* style, Irān, sixteenth century.

*Our thanks to the Cultural Institute of the I. R. of Irān in Italy
for the kind cooperation given to the relizaion of this work.*

© 2002 SEMAR PUBLISHERS SRL
VIA ARCO DI PARMA 18 • IT - 00186 ROME, ITALY
EMAIL info@semarweb.com
PO. BOX 40 • IT - 00100 ROME, ITALY
www.semarweb.com

*All rights reserved.
No part of this book
may be reproduced or transmitted
in any form by any means, media
and technologies existing now or
hereinafter developed, or by
any information storage
and retrieval system
without permission
in writing
from the Publisher.*

CONTENTS

❧

X
LIST OF PLATES
X
ACKNOWLEDGEMENTS
XI
NOTE ON TRANSLITERATION
XIII
FOREWORD BY PETER CHELKOWSKI
XVII
INTRODUCTION BY MOHAMMAD ʿALĪ MOVAHED
XXXIII
TRANSLATOR'S NOTE

DĪVĀN-I SHAMS-I TABRĪZ

3
I ≈ [14] - Lovers, O Lovers

7
II ≈ [74] - You Say: You are not a Seeker

9
III ≈ [94] - So much Love

11
IV ≈ [128] - Devoid of Self

13
V ≈ [132] - Within the Bloodied Caul

15
VI ≈ [163] - O Friends

17
VII ≈ [182] - Let There Be

19
VIII ≈ [189] - Spring is Here my Soul

23
IX ≈ [209] - You Who Knock at my Door

25
X ≈ [238] - For a Moment

27
XI ≈ [250] - Lo! I am at Your Threshold

XII = [328] - On Account of You — 31
XIII = [329] - Come, Come — 33
XIV = [330] - Once Again — 35
XV = [341] - Today is the Day — 39
XVI = [390] - O Leader of the Caravan — 41
XVII = [441] - Show your Face — 45
XVIII = [574] - For me a Lover is Such — 49
XIX = [595] - When you Have Love — 51
XX = [622] - How Can One — 53
XXI = [648] - O You, Who have Gone — 55
XXII = [649] - At Dawn — 57
XXIII = [650] - The One Who Appeared — 59
XXIV = [683] - If You Bake Bread — 61
XXV = [686] - O, Minstrel of the Soul — 63
XXVI = [874] - Look How the Dead — 65
XXVII = [911] - On the Day of My Death — 67
XXVIII = [1095] - My Love Put a Broom in my Hand — 69
XXIX = [1185] - I am so Drunk — 73
XXX = [1254] - I am You, You are I — 77
XXXI = [1311] - Once again — 79
XXXII = [1326] - Falling in Love — 81

XXXIII ≈ [1390] - I've Returned — *83*

XXXIV ≈ [1393] - I was Dead — *85*

XXXV ≈ [1439] - I don't Know this House — *89*

XXXVI ≈ [1447] - I Went to the Physician — *93*

XXXVII ≈ [1502] - I Liberated the People — *97*

XXXVIII ≈ [1516] - Your Soul is so Close — *101*

XXXIX ≈ [1517] - You Ask Me — *103*

XL ≈ [1519] - Come, for Today — *105*

XLI ≈ [1535] - Come, Let's Appreciate — *107*

XLII ≈ [1536] - Come Amongst Us — *109*

XLIII ≈ [1577] - Today I'm not Gloomy — *111*

XLIV ≈ [1585] - O World of Water and Mud — *113*

XLV ≈ [1586] - I Saw Myself as a Thorn — *115*

XLVI ≈ [1703] - I am the Black Night — *117*

XLVII ≈ [1810] - I Saw a Thief — *119*

XLVIII ≈ [2670] - Are You well, my Love? — *123*

NOTES — *125*

SELECTED BIBLIOGRAPHY — *133*

BIOGRAPHICAL NOTE — *137*

GLOSSARY — *139*

LIST OF PLATES

❖

PLATE *1*	One of the oldest portrait of Rūmī, and a calligraphic inscription *[Ya Hazrat Mowlānā, Praise be to Our Master, may God keep his secret]* in *nasta'līq* style, Īrān, sixteenth century.	*page*	IV
PLATE *2*	Zoomorphic *basmalah* on a Perisan marriage contract, dated 1760.	*page*	XII
PLATE *3*	Zoomorphic calligraphy, Shī'a prayer in *thuluth* style structured into the shape of a falcon, by Muhammad Fathiyāb, Īrān, early nineteenth century.	*page*	XVI
PLATE *4*	*Basmalah* in *thuluth* style, Īrān, ninetheenth century.	*page*	XXXII
PLATE *5*	Zoomorphic *basmalah* in the shape of a stork, Turkey, ninetheenth century.	*page*	124
PLATE *6*	Mirror *basmalah*, Turkey, ninetheenth century.	*page*	136

✦

ACKNOWLEDGMENTS

❖

*S*EVERAL *people deserve my gratitude for their support and guidance for the realization of this book. I would like to thank my old friend Sahlan Momo for publishing my translations and for his understanding and patience through the long work-in-progress. I am indebted to Murat Yagar and Marz Attar for their support. I would like to thank my daughter, Hedieh, and my friend Ralph Martin for their invaluable help. My deep appreciation goes to Jack Jurich who dedicated countless hours assisting me with editing and polishing English, and to Paul Glass for the final touches. To Mary Spidaletta and Ronnie Adler I owe my gratitude for their concern and encouragement. In the end, I would like to express my gratitude and love for my wife, Farrokh, who showed extreme loving patience, and to my young son, Sina, the sun of my life. Their presence was essential for the completion of this work.*

I.A.

✦

NOTE ON TRANSLITERATION

*D*IFFERENCES in the phonetic structure of Arabic and Persian make absolute consistency in transliteration impossible. The standard system used for Arabic (*Encyclopaedia of Islam*, 2nd ed.) with a few modifications works fine.

The following is a guide to the pronunciation of Persian words:

a	*a* as *man* in English;
ā	*ou* as *thought* in English;
e	*é* as *perché* in Italian;
i	*y* as *ally* in English;
ī	*ee* as *deer* in English;
dh	*th* as *this* in English;
gh	*g* as *luego* in Spansih;
h	always aspirate;
j	*j* as *John* in English;
kh	*ch* as *Nacht* in German;
ow	*ow* as *row* in English;
q	guttural sound as *kh*;
s	always voiceless;
sh	*sh* as *shall* in English;
th	*th* as *thing* in English;
z	always voiced;
ʿ	(*ʿayn*) occlusive glottal stop;
ʾ	(*hamza*) hiatus, not pronounced.

Zoomorphic Basmalah.
Īrān, seventeenth century.

FOREWORD

It is the fin de siecle, *therefore there must be a Persian poet on the horizon. And lo and behold, there is one: Rūmī.*

Towards the end of the nineteenth century, literary circles in England and America were under the spell of the Rubā'īyāt *of 'Omar Khayyām, the eleventh/twelfth century Persian poet. The epicureanism and skepticism of Khayyām, rendered so beautifully in English by Edward Fitzgerald, was, in the words of John D. Yohannan, a «consolation against a melancholy life» in Victorian England. Despite the many articles written by literary luminaries explaining the extraordinary success of the* Rubā'īyāt *in purely aesthetic terms, it was Khayyām's message itself which led to the formation of the popular 'Omar Khayyām Clubs of England and America. The cult of Khayyām faded away with the legend that his original manuscript, with its commentaries in his own hand written in the margins, had gone down to the bottom of the Atlantic Ocean with the Titanic.*

At this time of the new fin de siecle, *which also ushers in a new millenium, known as the age of globalization and the internet, another Persian poet reaches out his hands to humanity. It is Rūmī, the thirteenth-century Persian bard. He says:*

«Come, come again, wherever, whatever you may be,
Come, heathen, fire worshipper, sinful in idolatry, come.

> Come even if you have broken your penitence a hundred times,
> Ours is not the portal of despair and misery, come.»

The introduction of globalization and the internet were trumpeted as the roads leading to human happiness and harmony. But globalization did not eradicate the economic domination of the weak by the powerful. It did not bring racial, social, political and religious freedom. This genocidal century ended with yet other genocidal wars in the Balkans and in Central Africa, and with the ravagements of AIDS. In the thirteenth century, Rūmī championed his own vision of globalization, for which he was criticized. In response to his critics, he said:

> «What is this, O Muslims? I am lost. I am neither Christian nor Jew,
> Zoroastrian nor Muslim. I am neither from the East nor from the West,
> neither from the land nor the sea. I am not from India, China, Bulgaria
> or Spain, nor Irāq or Khorāsān. My place is no where. My home is no
> home. I have neither body nor soul. I am the soul of the Beloved.»

Here Rūmī negates the Self, and yet he says «There is nothing outside you in the universe. Seek within yourself for whatever you desire.»

Humankind has not changed in some seven hundred years since Rūmī's death; only the trappings of life have changed. The increasing multiplication and availability of media has created a bombardment which can easily give us the illusion that the whole world is spread before our feet like a carpet. And yet at the same time we cling to hundred-year-old barriers and feuds. Rūmī addresses these problems in simple, straight-forward language. He is a great poet, but poetic forms have no meaning for him.

What weighs with him is the message:

> «What on earth have I to do with 'poetry'?
> By God, I am fed up with poetic forms.
> They remind me of a man who thrusts his
> hand into tripe to clean it and cook
> it for a guest who loves a dish made of tripe!»

'Omar Khayyām had the good fortune to be rendered into English by Fitzgerald. Unfortunately, despite the growing hunger for Rūmī's poetry in English, he has yet to find his Fitzgerald.

The present volume, it is hoped, will bring Rūmī closer to English readers and narrow the gap between his powerful spiritual verse and its apprehension by those who have no Persian.

New York, May 2001.

PETER CHELKOWSKI

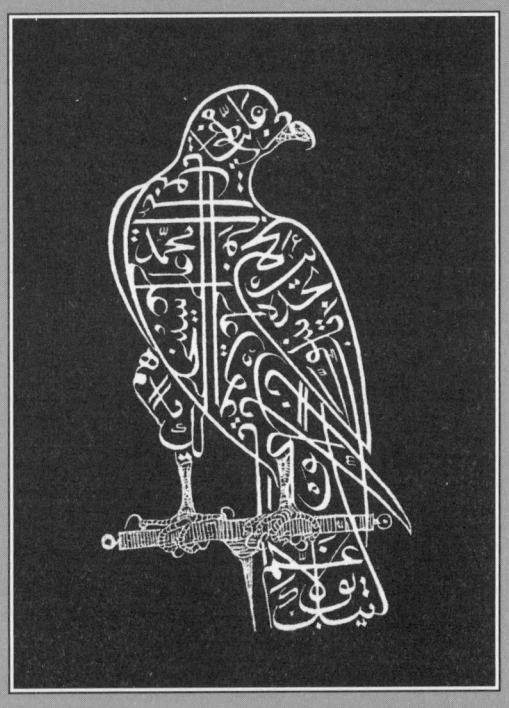

Zoomorphic calligraphy,
Īrān, seventeenth century.

INTRODUCTION

> «*I have been told that:*
> *"This beautiful servant of ours*
> *is captive among this rough*
> *crowd. It would be a pity if*
> *they bring him to harm."*»[1]

BY EXAMINING THE WORK OF RŪMĪ WE REALIZE WE ARE DEALING NOT only with one person and three different voices, but one person and three different personas:

a) Rūmī before joining Shams;
b) Rūmī of the time of rapture and bewilderment, drowned in the «Magic of Shams-i Tabrīz;»[2]
c) the tamed Rūmī, calmed and calming as a mountain, tall as the sky with a wide spread skirt, compassionate, kind and protective.

Shams-i Tabrīz arrived in Konya on the morning of Saturday, the twenty-sixth of the month of Jamādi al Ākhir[3] of the year 642 A.H. / 29[b] of November 1244 A.D.. This date has been registered, with precision in different versions of the Māqalāt, in Persian and Arabic[d]. This event occurred about fourteen or fifteen years after Rūmī's father, Bahā-ad-dīn Walad, died. Mowlānā[5] Jalāl-ad-dīn[6] Rūmī was then a middle-aged man, about forty years old[f]. He had completed his education many years before with well-known teachers in Aleppo and Damascus. His father bore the grandiose title of Sultān-ul-'Ulamā (King of the theologians). He had the ultimate rank of fatwā and irshād (judgment and guidance), meaning, although he wore the robe of the faqīh (theologian) and was considered an expert in religious sciences, he also had a great name among the followers of the tarīqa (the path of the Islamic mystics) *and sūfī leaders. Sultān-ul-'Ulamā lived in Balkh, which he left around the time of the Mongol invasion. After having made the pilgrimage of Mecca he went to Asia Minor, which was then called Bilād-al Rūm[8], where he and his followers established themselves in the city of Konya, the capital of the Saljuq king, Alā-ad-dīn Kayqubād (617-634 A.H. / 1220-1236 A.D.). In each town or village the Mongols arrived, killed everyone, looted everything and burned whatever remained. Therefore, it is not a surprise that whoever had a horse or a donkey would mount and ride from the danger zone. The mass-flight from the horrors of the Mongol invasion was not only by the wealthy and powerful, but also by scientists, writers and other artists.*

In the biography of Sultān-ul-'Ulamā, it is mentioned that every morning he had a majlis-i dars *(teching session), and on Monday and Friday he would go to the pulpit and preach to his followers. Before knowing Shams, Mowlānā Jalāl ad-dīn Rūmī had chosen to continue the life style of his father, and, since he was younger and more energetic, his activities and stamina were obviously greater. Documents indicate that he taught in four of Konya's theological schools. Contributing to his prosperity as a cleric, he had a pulpit in a mosque, where his followers gathered. The core of his followers consisted of the initiated entourage of Sultān-ul Ulamā, which had left Khurāsān for Bilād-al Rūm about twenty years before, following their master and teacher.*

The arrival of Shams in Konya turned Rūmī's orderly and peaceful life completely upside down and provoked a hurricane in his soul that did not stop haunting him for the rest of his life. From this hurricane rose the Mowlānā Rūmī whom we know – the Rūmī whose warmth of utterance, the agitation of his flowing thought, and the unique passion and captivating quality of his word can be seen in the Dīvān-i Shams *and the* Mathnavī. *After the appearance of Shams, Mowlānā rejected official prestige, and that which appeared proper and pleasing to his followers' eyes. He left the* madrisa *and the pulpit, relinquishing the chair of* fatwā *to others. Rūmī was no longer the man his followers knew. His life had gone through a drastic upheaval. He was journeying in another universe. He was trapped in a snare and he could not see a way out of it, and said:*

> «When *Shams-ul Haq-i Tabrīz* draws you in his snare
> do not look left or right, there is no way to avoid it!»

Shams-i Tabrīz had set fire to his existence[9]. In this bewildering hurricane, the dignified sheikh of the city became so disheveled and ruined that his followers were amazed and friends became strangers. He had no concern for his good name and no fear of others.

> «If the good name is gone, less to worry about.
> The place of the lover is outside of air and water.
> If friends turn away from me,
> the friend of the swimmer is the sea.»[10]

❁

What happened between Mowlānā and Shams in their first encounter, which began such a radical transformation? Of the accounts that have reached us, the story of Fereydūn Sepahsālār appears the most reliable. In his book he emphasizes that for forty years, day and night, he has been a companion and in the service of Mowlānā, and has been like: «[...] a compass with [his] head on the point of his threshold.»[11] Mowlānā died in A.H. 672 / 1274 A.D.. If we deduct forty years from this date we get 1234. When Shams arrived in Konya in 1244, it would have been approximately ten years that Sepahsālār had been serving Mowlānā. He should be considered one of his oldest followers. His book and the Ibtidā nāmeh *of Sultān Walad, the youngest son of Rūmī, are first hand documents available for research on the life of Rūmī and his relationship with Shams.*

The following is the story of Mowlānā's first encounter with Shams, depicted by Sepahsālār: «Shams went to Konya dressed as a merchant and took residence in the caravanserai of the rice sellers. Outside the caravanserai there were elegant platforms, where the dignitaries of the city gathered to socialize. One morning, Shams was sitting on a platform and Mowlānā was approaching in a circle of his followers; people were rushing from every direction to kiss Mowlānā's hand for blessing and he "comforted and treated everyone kindly." When Mowlānā reached the platform he saw Shams and *stopped and sat on another platform opposite Shams. The two looked at each other for a while without speaking. Then Shams raised his head and addressed Rūmī: "Mowlānā, may God have compassion on you [...]." And Shams asked about Bāyazīd, who never ate melon in his life because he said he had never seen any saying about the Prophet eating melon. Such a man, who was so meticulous in following the Prophet, states "Subhāni mā a'd-hamu sh'ani,"[12] and: "Laytha fī jubbatī illallāh."[13] Whereas the Prophet with all his greatness and glory said: "Sometimes I feel turmoil in my heart and ask God seventy times a day for His forgiveness."»[14] The answer of Mowlānā, according to Sepahsālār, was that Bāyazīd reached a specific status in the circle of walāyat[15]. There he remained in the face of the greatness and the perfection of that status; he was overwhelmed and made those statements because his perception could not see beyond his state. In contrast, the Prophet never stopped his process of perfection. Everyday he would surpass seventy great spiritual stations and found each station low and worthless, relative to the next station; so he would ask forgiveness for having lingered, even for one extra moment in that lower station.*

After this conversation, Sepahsālār relates that Shams and Mowlānā descended from the platform, shook hands and embraced. Then «[...] for a period of six months they kept each other company, in the cell of sheikh Salāh-ad-dīn Zarkūb.» During this time they would not permit anyone to disturb their privacy except sheikh Salāh-ad-dīn.

When their seclusion came to an end Mowlānā set aside his turban and robes of the high clergy and dressed like Shams[16]. Sepahsālār makes it clear that until that time «[...] he had never done samā'.»[17] Shams ordered him to do samā': «Begin the samā'. What you seek will increase in samā'.»

> «He said: "You are a sheikh, a head, a guide and a leader."
> I am not a sheikh, a leader. I am a slave to your command.
> You are the source of the sun. I am the shade of the willow.
> Since your rays have fallen upon my head, humble and molten I became.»[18]

To hear this story is easy, but is not so easy to see a dignified praying sheikh[19], who has been teaching the religious sciences, in a state of samā' and dance. Shams understood Mowlānā's dilemma and was trying to placate him with theological language: «[...] samā' *has been declared forbidden for the common people because they are using it to gratify the self. When they do* samā,' *that despised and abominable state intensifies and they move out of self-amusement and vanity. Consequently, for these people* samā' *is forbidden. On the other hand, those who are seekers, in love with God and heed nothing but God will have that state and longing increased. Therefore,* samā' *is allowed to this people.»[20] The persuasive words of Shams convinced Mowlānā; he obeyed the order of the* pīr[21] *and according to Sepahsālār: «He acted in that fashion and made it his way and rite till the end of his life.»[22]*

Aflāki's account of this story corresponds in general with Sepahsālār. There are only slight differences in the details. For example, the name of the place where Shams resided was the «Caravanserai of the sugar sellers.» According to Aflāki, on that day Mowlānā had just left the «School of Cotton sellers» and was among his followers when Shams saw him passing by the caravanserai of the sugar sellers. He got up and took the reins of Mowlānā's mount and said: «O, leader of the Muslims, was Bāyazīd greater or Muḥammad?»

It seems that the name of this caravanserai had been changed between the time of Aflāki and Sepahsālār. Aflāki finished his book in 754 A.H. / 1353 A.D., one hundred and twenty years after the events under discussion. Apparently, the caravanserai known as the «rice sellers» at the time of Sepahsālār later had become the caravanserai of the «sugar sellers».

❁

Shams-i Tabrīz stayed in Konya for sixteen months, then packed and left. The exact date of this departure, written by the hand of Mowlānā and recorded by Husām-ad-dīn Chalabi, is Thursday, 21ˢᵗ of Shavvāl of the year 643 A.H. / 11ᵗʰ of November 1246 A.D.[23] Shams undertook this voyage as a protest. He was extremely disheartened by the trouble and conflict created by Mowlānā's followers. They said: «Who is this unknown man who has just arrived and has led astray the sheikh *of the city, the son of Sultān-ul-'Ulamā? Who is this man who has conquered the mind and the thought of the most knowledgeable man of the time and ruined his life?» Sultān Walad, son of Mowlānā, depicts the mindset of the followers in this way:*

> «Perhaps he is a sorcerer and by sorcery
> has drawn our sheikh into his seductive snare.
> Otherwise who is he and what is in him?
> How can he live with this trickery?
> No one knows his origin or family.
> We don't even know where he comes from.»[24]

Sultān Walad, Sepahsālār and Aflāki, all believe that misplaced jealousy and ignorant fanaticism were the source of this animosity. Mowlānā's followers truly loved him and their extreme feelings of attachment fueled their fanaticism, making them act arrogantly and speak foolishly. Shams deemed it prudent to leave Mowlānā to his followers and get away from Konya. This was a colossal test, which left Mowlānā to look within himself, without the charisma of Shams, and perhaps to revert to his old life and habits.

The followers hoped for this but it did not come to pass. As long as Shams was in Konya the magnet of his presence drew Mowlānā to him and now that he was gone the pain of yearning flooded the soul of Mowlānā and disabled him. Mowlānā was deeply and bitterly distraught and heartbroken. The pīr of Tabrīz *was gone and had taken Mowlānā's mind with him. The joy of life had left him and he could not tolerate anybody or anything. Friend and foe seemed as one to him. According to Sepahsālār: «Khudāvandgār*[25] *cut off all his followers and went into seclusion. In addition, the rest of the companions and loved ones were helpless with regard to the actions of those people [the opponents of Shams].»*[26] *A strange situation developed. The followers were confused and regretful, blaming themselves for what they had done. The gossip mongers and agitators had begun to apologize.*

Finally, the consternation and confusion of Mowlānā came to an end and there appeared a crack in the silent wall of hopelessness and boredom that was oppressing the atmosphere of Konya. A messenger came from Damascus and delivered a letter from the pīr of Tabrīz *to Mowlānā. Now it was clear where the* pīr *was and that his heart faced Mowlānā. The fire under the ashes rose again and shone. Again Mowlānā returned to the universe of passion, poetry and* samāʿ. *He described his state poetically in a few ghazals, which he entrusted with some money to his son, Sultān Walad, and sent him, with a group of intimate friends, to Damascus to relay his longing and the regret of his followers to Shams. Following his father's order to persuade Shams to return at any cost to Konya, Sultān Walad convinced Shams to do so*[27]. *Shams understood the need of Mowlānā and returned to Konya with Sultān Walad. The journey lasted about a month. Walad, out of respect for Shams, walked the entire way in his service. He recounts the story:*

> «Walad walked the road in his service,
> not out of necessity, but with sincerity and from his soul.
> The King told him: «You also mount a horse,
> that gentle gray one».
> Walad replied: «O, King of Kings
> I cannot endure being your equal.
> How can the King ride and the slave also?
> This is not correct, do not say, beware!
> It is necessary that I walk on foot.
> To be in your service I would run on my head».
> More than one month he walked on foot,
> without rest, at times descending, and others ascending.
> Although the way was arduous, it came easily,
> for, the hardship unlocked the treasure's lock.»[28]

At Shams' arrival the followers rejoiced; they prepared feasts and celebrations and brought many gifts. Shams forgave them and with his sweet words the circle of Mowlānā acquired a new atmosphere. Now Shams married a beautiful young girl, Kimya, who, according to Sepahsālār, had grown up in the house of Mowlānā under the supervision of Gerāy Khatūn, Mowlānā's wife. Mowlānā arranged for the pīr *of Tabrīz and his young wife to reside in his house and there they spent the winter of that year.*

But the calm of the followers and the patience of the gossip mongers did not last long. It was a calm that had a horrific hurricane behind it. Soon, using Sultān Walad's words «The deceit of the Devil» emerged and calumny began here and there and malice took effect. Shams threatened that this time he would go without leaving a trace. Sepahsālār quotes Shams: «This time [...] I will disappear so that no creature can find a trace of me.»[29] Sultān Walad has a similar account:

> «This time I will leave in such a way
> that no one will know where I am.
> Everyone will be helpless in the search,
> no one will ever see any trace of me.
> Thus, countless years will pass
> and no one will find any sign of my dust.»[30]

And that is what came to pass: one Thursday morning of the year 645 A.H. / 1248 A.D., when Mowlānā went to the theological school to see the pīr «[...] he found the abode empty.»[31] Shams had acted upon his threat and left Konya. When, how and where did he go? Nobody knew. Sultān Walad states: «Suddenly he disappeared from the midst of all.»[32] Sepahsālār more politely articulates: «Suddenly, he went into occultation.»[33] That is all, nothing else! Shams's custom was not to settle down. He would go from town to town and as soon as he would be recognized and people gathered around him, he would pack and run. For this reason he was called «The Flying Shams.»[34] Sepahsālār states: «Hazrat-i Khudāvandgār[35] [Rūmī] roared like a cloud.»[36] But what good would moaning and weeping do? It was thought that, once again, Shams had gone to Syria and taken residence in Aleppo or Damascus. Mowlānā inquired after him with every traveler from Syria, and journeyed there too, but found no sign of Shams.

It is not clear what happened to Shams after he left Konya. His tomb has been reported in different places, among which are Konya, Khoy and Tabrīz. As time passed more legends were created: some said that Shams' enemies had killed him in Konya and thrown his body in a well. This account, with all the popularity it has gained, is not believable. It may have been taken from among the words uttered by Shams himself: «I will go and after awhile when there is no news of me they will say: "He must certainly have been killed somewhere."»[37]

In those days Konya was too small for a murder — and for that matter the murder of Shams — to have remained hidden. Frequent trips by Mowlānā to Syria in search of Shams demonstrate this story has been fabricated at a later date. The elegies by Mowlānā that exist in the Dīvān-i Shams *tell about his natural death.*

In my opinion, Shams, after having left Konya, headed for Tabrīz and on this journey or while returning to Syria died on the road.

The shrine that is being made in honor of Shams in Khoy is probably his true resting place.

Tradition wanted students and followers to take notes of the words of the sheikhs and pīrs *in their gatherings.* Maqālāt-i Shams *is a collection of such notes. Aflākī had one of these collections in his possession and has related a selection in the fourth chapter and other parts of his book. After Aflākī, it is rare to find a trace of the* Maqālāt. *Among Iranian researchers of our time, the late Badi'uzamān-i Furūzānfar is the first who worked on one of the versions of the* Maqālāt *and was captivated by: «[...] the subtlety of the phrases and beauty of the words.»[38] Furūzānfar considered the* Maqālāt *one of the treasures of Persian literature and the key to understanding the thoughts of Rūmī. Before the discovery of the* Maqālāt *it was difficult to speak in scholarly terms about Shams. Some did not believe in his existence and considered him a figment of Rūmī's imagination. The famous iranologist, Edward Browne, quoting from Nicholson[39], presents Shams as an illuminated* pīr *but uneducated[40]. The* Maqālāt *proves the opposite of these statements and clarifies that Shams was an erudite scholar. He was extremely familiar with the holy Qur'ān and his incisive comments and mastery of its mystical interpretation is miraculous. He had studied* fiqh[41]; *he had associated with the luminaries and the great men in the mystical milieu who were his contemporaries. In short, he was well versed in all the sciences of his time. And let us not forget that those were the days the blossoming of Islamic mysticism was at its height. Sepahsālār states that, according to Mowlānā, he knew some mathematics and astronomy.*

«*It is undeniable that the most mysterious chapter of the life of Mowlānā is his relationship with Shams-i Tabrīz [...] now the* Maqālāt *unveils many of these mysteries and to a certain extent explains the rapture of Mowlānā for Shams and, contrary to accepted wisdom, presents him as a knowledgeable seer and lover of Truth, therefore worthy of being a leader and a guide.*»[42] Shams ascribes going to Konya to orders from beyond and states clearly that this journey was because of Mowlānā: «*I have been told that: "this beautiful servant of ours is captive among this rough crowd. It would be a pity if they bring him to harm."*»[43] Mowlānā, that beautiful servant, would be elevated to the exalted position of 'friend' of God from a mere clergyman and teacher. Shams had come to make a saint out of a preacher. Considering his words in another instance, it is understood that he had been eying Mowlānā for a long time but had not yet deemed him worthy of his companionship: «*I pleaded with the Almighty: "let me be a companion and close to your friends."* [44] *I was told: "We shall make you a companion with one friend." I said: "Where is that friend?" Next night I saw and I was told: "He is in* Rūm.*" When I saw after a long time, I was told: "It is not time yet. Everything has its proper time."*»[45]

In another instance Shams states: «*My attraction to you was powerful from the beginning. But I saw in your initial word that you were not worthy of these mysteries. If I talked, it would have been absurd and this moment would be lost.*»[46]

Apparently he had known Mowlānā for fifteen or sixteen years since Mowlānā had been a young student. In those days, in Damascus, he walked behind his father, Sultān-ul-ʿUlamā; and in his company he associated with great ṣūfīs such as Muhyīddīn Ibn ʿArabī, Saʿd-ad-dīn Humavi, Uʿthmān-i Rūmī, Awhad-ad-dīn-i Kirmāni and Sadr-ad-dīn-i Qawnawi. Of this time lapse of fifteen or sixteen years there are four references in the Maqālāt[47]. Further, in two places of Manāqib-al ʿĀrifīn, Aflākī mentions a previous encounter between Rūmī and Shams in Damascus[48], which is related from the «Ancient friends,» meaning the old followers of Rūmī who depicted Shams in the midst of people as a «*Strange man [...] with a black felt robe and a black hat.» Mowlānā takes his hand and states: «Purifier of the world, save me!»*[49] *But Shams goes into the crowd and disappears.*

In various spots of the Maqālāt, where Shams mentions Sultān-ul-'Ulamā and his intimate followers, the tone of his words illustrates his acquaintance with them. Also his sayings about sayyed Burhān-ad-dīn Muhaqqeq who, after Sultān-ul-'Ulamā, was Mowlānā's teacher and spiritual mentor, tell us about his previous association with them. It seems that Shams met this crowd after they went to Syria and Asia Minor. There is no doubt that Shams frequented the gatherings of the mystics but rarely showed his true self [50]. He would go around in merchant's clothes and would avoid residing in madrasas and khaniqāhs; to earn a living he would teach in the maktabs[51] or work as a hired hand, hiding his true status. He was one of the «auwliyā-yi mastūr»[52] of God who avoided fame and being revealed. He states: «I have nothing to do with the commoners in this world. I have not come for them.» «I have not talked with anyone except Mowlānā.»[53] «I do not take murīds[54]. They insisted to be my followers but I ran [...] I do not take murīds. I take sheikhs, and not just any sheikh, only perfect sheikhs.»[55]

In the Maqālāt, addressing a certain sheikh Ibrāhīm, who had been a follower of Sultān-ul-'Ulamā, he states: «Whoever hears a word from me, it is by the blessings of Mowlānā. Does anybody ever hear anything from me? Did I ever say anything to anyone? You are Ibrāhīm who would come to school; you would see me only as a teacher! But there are many who serve in hiding. There is an enormous difference between serving in appearance and [serving] in hiding.»[56] According to Mowlānā, the pīr of Tabrīz loved sheikh Ibrāhīm. They had been friends for years, but Shams's spiritual status remained beyond the comprehension of sheikh Ibrāhīm. He would visit Shams at school and see him as a mere grammar school teacher.

This is how the Maqālāt introduces Shams: «An old man with a faint beard and thin body who appears weak but is nimble and lively. His speech is pleasant and incisive; he is extremely self-reliant and self-controlled, with *complete belief and confidence in his position. He does not care about worldly protocols and customs. He is magnanimous, self-contained and introverted, but full of passion, restless, stinging, quarrelsome and direct, a man who can sit silent for hours and listen, but if he speaks he will not allow any argument. He appreciates the official sciences but he considers them useless, even obtrusive. He is not fond of ceremonies and rites of the orthodox sūfīs, but he believes that walking on the path of* tarīqa *needs guidance and leadership. He is lenient, polite and tolerant towards strangers, but he is not satisfied with a friend unless he absolutely submits. His expectation from a friend is enormous: infinite sacrifice.»*

These are the main characteristics of the man whose influence and magical dominance over Mowlānā Jalāl-ad-dīn Rūmī did not leave him even for a moment in the last thirty years of his life.

Moḥammad ʿAlī Movahed

[*Translation by Iraj Anvar*]

•

---

[1] *Maqālāt-i Shams-i Tabrīz*, Intishārāt-i Khārazmi, Tehran 1989, p. 622.

[2] This is one of Rūmī's own expressions.

[3] The 6th month of the Islamic year.

[4] *Maqālāt…, op. cit.*, p. 68.

[5] *Mowlānā* is an honorific title, meaning «Our lord». In Persian, Rūmī is commonly called *Mowlānā* in the same way the Turkish people call him *Mevlānā*. The writer of this introduction constantly uses *Mowlānā*. I took the liberty of using Rūmī in some instances, for the sake of the Western reader. [*I.A.*].

[6] Jalāl-ad-dīn is the first name of Rūmī.

[7] AFLĀKĪ, *Manāqib al-Ārifīn,* corrections by Tahsīn Yāzjīī, Historical Turkish Society, Ankara 1959, vol. 2, p. 618. «In those days, Hazrat-i Mowlānā [His excellency, our Lord] was teaching religious sciences and taught in the four major *madrisas* (religious schools).»

[8] Regions of Rome. All the territories on the West of Persia were considered Rome, without discrimination, including Asia Minor. Therefore, Rūmī literally means Roman.

[9] «*From afar I saw Shams (the sun) of the soul,*
the pride of Tabrīz and the envy of China.
That apple of the eye of the Heavens,
that reviver of the earth.
He set fire to my existence,
he uprooted vanity and hatred.»

BADI'UZAMĀN-I FURŪZĀNFAR, *Kulliyyāt-i Shams-i Tabrīz*, Teheran 1958-1968, vol. I, Ghazal 117.

[10] *Ibidem*, vol. I, Ghazal 497.

[11] FEREYDŪN SEPAHSĀLĀR, *Risāleh-ī Sepahsalar,* Ganipoor, A.H.1319 / A.D. 1901, p. 17.

[12] Saying «*subhān allāh*» is to praise the Almighty. *Subhān* is also used to express amazement. What Bāyazīd says means that he is amazed by the greatness of his own stature.

[13] Bāyazīd is reported to have said: «There is no one in my cloak but God.»

[14] This is a *hadīth*, a saying of the Prophet. [*I.A.*].

[15] *Walāyat* comes from *walī* and is a high spiritual status. According to sūfī doctrine, a *walī* is a friend of God and his/her will is the will of God. [*I.A.*].

[16] Shams wore an outfit of black felt and a black sash on his head. Mowlānā's appearance is described: «Medium height, gray hair, yellow complexion, black sash on the head and a robe made of striped Indian linen.» AFLĀKĪ, *op.cit.* vol. II, p. 612.

[17] Literal meaning of *samā'* is «to listen» but in the sūfī tradition it refers to ritualistic dance accompanied by spiritual music. [*I.A.*].

[18] BADI'UZAMĀN-I FURŪZĀNFAR, *Kulliyyāt-i Shams...* cit., vol. IV. Ghazal 1393.

[19] This refers to a couplet of Rūmī:
«*I was a dignified praying man,*
You made me a plaything for the street children.»

[20] Sepahsālār has related these words from Shams to convince Rūmī to do *samā'.* SEPAHSĀLĀR, *op. cit.,* p. 32.

[21] Spiritual teacher and guide. [*I.A.*].

[22] SEPAHSĀLĀR, *op. cit..*

[23] AFLĀKĪ, *op. cit,* vol. II, p. 629.

[24] SULTĀN WALAD, *Ibtidā nameh (Walad nameh)*, correction by Jalāl Homāī, Intishārāt-i Iqbāl, A.H. 1315 / A.D. 1898, p. 43.

[25] One of the titles of Rūmī, meaning «lord».

[26] SEPAHSĀLĀR, *op. cit.*, p. 66.

[27] According to AFLĀKĪ (*Manāqib ...*, vol. II, p. 688) Shams twice left Konya for Damascus, in anger, and it was the second time that Rūmī sent his son to fetch him. Sepahsālār and Sultān Walad have not said a word about Shams' first departure. Here is the account of Aflāki:

«It is related from knowledgeable followers that the first time Hazrat-i Mowlānā Shams-ad-dīn went to Damascus, it was because of the jealousy of the faithless jealous ones and the enmity of the doubtful ignoble ones. After a long stay he returned by request of Mowlānā and honored Konya [with his presence], keeping close company [with Mowlānā] for several months. Again the worthless envious ones became enraged and made the wide world narrow for them. On his second disappearance, Hazrat-i Mowlānā, out of the benevolence for his beloved son, ordered him to travel to Damascus with twenty enlightened ones to seek Shams-ad-dīn, may God glorify his memory.»

Hazrat is a title of honor. We see in this quote, Mowlānā, meaning our Lord, is used for both Shams and Rūmī. But the name *Shams* always appears after it to refer to Shams while, when *Mowlānā* stands alone, it refers specifically to Rūmī. [*I.A.*].

[28] *Ibtidā nameh, op. cit.*, p. 49.

[29] SEPAHSĀLĀR, *op. cit.*, p. 69.

[30] *Ibtidā nameh*, p. 52.

[31] SEPAHSĀLĀR, *op. cit.*, p. 69.

[32] *Ibtidā nameh, op.cit.*, p. 52.

[33] SEPAHSĀLĀR, *op. cit.*, p . 69.

[34] *Shams-i parandeh.*

[35] See footnote 25.

[36] SEPAHSĀLĀR, *op. cit.*, p. 69.

[37] *Ibtidā nameh, op.cit.*, p. 52.

Such many years will pass,
no one will find any sign of my dust.
When a long time goes by they will say:
Certainly an enemy killed him.

[38] BADI'UZAMĀN-I FURŪZĀNFAR, *Risāleh Dar Tahqiq-i Ahwāl va Zindigāni-i Mowlānā Jalāl-ad-dīn Muhammad* [The life and time of Rūmī], Teheran 1954, vol. II, p. 90.

[39] R.A. Nicholson dedicated a great part of his life to Rūmī's work. He translated the entire *Mathnawī* and wrote a commentary on it. He also translated a selection of his *Ghazals* from the *Ghazaliyāt-i Shams*. [*I.A.*].

[40] E.G. BROWNE, *A literary History of Persia*, Cambridge 1951-1953, vol. II, p. 517.

[41] Islamic jurisprudence. [*I.A.*].

[42] BADI'UZAMĀN-I FURŪZĀNFAR, *Kulliyyāt-i Shams*... cit., p. 89.

[43] *Maqālāt, op. cit.*, p. 622.

[44] *Awliyā* [plural of *walī*]. See footnote 9 of this «Introduction». In this quote *walī* has been replaced with *friend* in all instances. [*I.A.*].

[45] *Maqālāt, op. cit.*, p. 60-759.

[46] *Ibidem*, p. 19-618.

[47] *Ibidem*, pp. 290; 690; 734; 763.

[48] AFLĀKĪ, *op. cit.*, vol. I, p. 82; and vol. II, p. 618.

[49] *Sarrāf-i' ālam*, literally «The money changer of the world». [*I.A.*].

[50] In a letter that survived Shams, we read: «I visited many precious *dervishes* and profited from their presence. And the difference between the true and the false became clear, both through word and by deed [...] This bird does not pick just any seed». *Maqālāt*, p. 784.

[51] Children's school. [*I.A.*].

[52] Hidden saints. [*I.A.*].

[53] *Maqālāt*, p. 739.

[54] Follower. [*I.A.*].

[55] *Maqālāt*, p. 226.

[56] *Ibidem*, p. 729.

✦

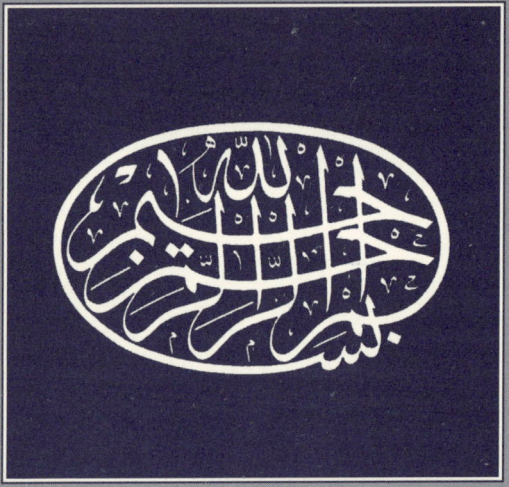

Basmalah, Īrān, nineteenth century.

TRANSLATOR'S NOTE

❧

I have known Rūmī all my life. When I was a baby my father would sing Rūmī's Masnavī to calm me. This is not a privilege I claim only for myself since countless Iranians become familiar with Rūmī and other great poets early in life. After I learned some European languages, I dreamed for years about translating Rūmī. Then, fifteen years ago I agreed with Semar to realize my dream. But the project was postponed since I dared not tamper with Rūmī's language after having read many translations which left me disappointed. Later, I discovered it was not only the quality of the translations but my failure to be able to read them from a non-Persian point of view: I was always trying to translate them back into Persian. Of course that didn't work and I would feel compelled to return to the original poetry, which reinforced my conviction that any attempt I might make translating Rūmī or other poets, such as Ḥāfiz would betray the original. So I decided to let this 'sin' be committed by others.

In 1994, the fine poet Elizabeth Gray asked me to work with her on her translations of fifty *ghazals* of Ḥāfiz, which she had achieved long ago and were finally scheduled for publication. Although I had been teaching Rūmī, Ḥāfiz and other Persian poets for some years at New York University, and studying and discussing them almost daily, I had not yet been involved with a translation for publication. The few months I worked with Elizabeth proved a revelation: not only did I learn a great deal about English poetry and, wonder of wonders, Persian poetry, I began to appreciate how the former can be a relatively faithful reflection of the latter. Soon I gave renewed consideration to translating Rūmī into English. But being a procrastinator by nature, I delayed once again until one evening, three years ago, my eccentric friend, Ben Hume, called and expressed his frustration about a Rūmī translation he had read; according to him, it denigrated our poet. Ben argued I had a duty to translate Rūmī because of my fluency with Persian, my familiarity with the material, and, not least, my love for the poet. He stressed I owed it to Rūmī to reveal his work in the way I understood him. Ben touched me and I felt compelled to begin that very night.

Although I love poetry, I am not a poet. My method has been an attempt to convey the thoughts and ideas of the Master by treating form secondary to content. When I began choosing *ghazals* for this edition, I browsed through the *Dīvan-i Shams-i Tabrīz* and considered the most attractive theme to be the constant confrontation of love (*'ishq*) and reason (*'aql*). Then, I realized there were *ghazals* I admired which had different themes and I decided they must be included. Not stopping there, I chose *ghazals* with surrealistic images and outrageous concepts, which may seem blasphemous to orthodox mentality. Some *ghazals* have been chosen by my writer friend, 'Alī Morad Fadainia, my musician/painter friend, Reza Derakhshānī, and my wife, Farrokh. The version of the *Dīvān* I used is the *Dīvān-i Shams-i Tabrīz* by Badi'uzamān-i Furūzānfar [Teheran 1958-1968]. I also consulted the selections of Mohammad Reza Shafiī-ye Kadkani, *Gozīdeh-ye Ghazaliyāt-e Shams* [Tehran 1378 / 1999, 12th ed.]. Several *bayts* were omitted since, I thought, they would require extensive footnotes, of which there are already, perhaps, too many; some others were omitted to avoid repetition. To present these *ghazals* in simple and modern English, accessible to any Western reader, has been one of my goals. Nevertheless, ambiguities have been rendered as much as possible without notation, leaving each reader to decipher hidden or obscure meanings.

I.A

❂

Dīvān-i Shams-i Tabrīz

FORTY-EIGHT GHAZALS

۱-[۱۴] - ای عاشقان ای عاشقان امروز ماییم و شما

۱ ای عاشقان ای عاشقان امروز ماییم و شما
افتاده در غرقابه‌ای تا خود که داند آشنا

۲ گر سیل عالم پر شود هر موج چون اشتر شود
مرغان ابی را چه غم تا غم خورد مرغ هوا

۳ ما رخ ز شکر افروخته با موج و بحر آموخته
زان سان که ماهی را بود دریا و طوفان جان فزا

۴ این باد اندر هر سری سودای دیگر می‌پزد
سودای آن ساقی مرا باقی همه آن شما

۵ دیروز مستان را به ره بربود آن ساقی کُله
امروز می در می‌دهد تا بر کند از ما قبا

۶ ای رشک ماه و مشتری با ما و پنهان چون پری
خوش خوش کشانم می‌بری آخر نگویی تا کجا؟

۷ هر جا روی تو با منی ای هردو چشم و روشنی
خواهی سوی مستیم کش خواهی ببر سوی فنا

۸ عالم چو کوه طور دان ما همچو موسی طالبان
هر دم تجلّی می‌رسد بر می‌شکافد کوه را

DĪVĀN-I SHAMS-I TABRĪZ

I ≈ [14] - *LOVERS, O LOVERS*

⚜

1. *L*OVERS, O lovers, you and I are here, today,
   cast into a whirlpool. Let us see who will stay afloat.

2. If water were to flood the world, with waves high as camels
   the seabird will love that water. Let the shorebirds worry.

3. My face is lit with gratitude, I'm one with the waves and the sea,
   like the fish, thriving on rain and storm.

4. In each head this wind brews a different madness…
   The passion for the *sāqi*[1] is mine. You can have the rest.

5. Yesterday, on the road, the hats of the drunkards were the
   [*sāqi*'s catch.
   Today, filling us with wine, he comes for our cloaks.

6. O envy of the moon and Jupiter, amongst us, yet hidden like
   [the fairies.
   You're gently drawing me away. To where, won't you say?

7. Wherever You go I go with You, O light of my eyes.
   Take me to the wine, take me to annihilation, as You wish.

8. Think of the world as mount Sinai, and think of us as seekers,
   [such as Moses.
   Each moment there is a revelation, shattering the mountain.

یک پاره اخضر میشود یک پاره عبهر می شود
یک پاره گوهر می شود یک پاره لعل و کهربا

ای طالب دیدار او بنگر در این کهسار او
ای کُه چه باده خورده ای؟ ما مست گشتیم از صدا

ای باغبان ای باغبان در ما چه در پیچیده ای؟
گر برده ایم انگور تو تو برده ای انبان ما

9 One part becomes leaf, the other blossom.
  One part becomes pearl, the others ruby and amber.
10 You, who long to see His Countenance, look upon His [mountain².
  O mountain, what wine have you drunk? We are drunk [with echoes.
11 O keeper of the vineyard, why grapple with me?
  True, I stole your grape, but you took my skin.

گر زانکه نئی طالب جوینده شوی با ما

۱. گر زانکه نئی طالب جوینده شوی با ما
    ور زانکه نئی مطرب گوینده شوی با ما
۲. گر زانکه تو قارونی در عشق شوی مفلس
    ور زانکه خداوندی هم بنده شوی با ما
۳. یک شمع از این مجلس صد شمع بگیراند
    گر مرده ای ور زنده هم زنده شوی با ما
۴. پا های تو بگشاید روشن بتو بنماید
    تا تو همه تن چون گل درخنده شوی با ما
۵. در ژنده درآ یک دم تا زنده دلان بینی
    اطلس بدر اندازی در ژنده شوی با ما
۶. چون دانه شد افکنده بر رست و درختی شد
    این رمز چو دریابی افکنده شوی با ما
۷. شمس الحق تبریزی با غنچهٔ دل گوید
    چون باز شود چشمت بیننده شوی با ما

II = [74] - *YOU SAY: YOU ARE NOT A SEEKER*

1. You say: you are not a seeker. With us you'll become one.
And if you're not a minstrel, with us you will sing.
2. If you are the richest[1], in love, you'll be bankrupt;
and if a lord, with us you'll be a slave.
3. One candle from this crowd will light a thousand candles.
Whether you are dead or alive, with us you will live.
4. Your feet unshackled, the way clearly revealed,
your whole being will laugh, like a rose in bloom.
5. Come, dress in rags for a moment and see the light;
then you'll throw away the silks and wear rags with us.
6. The fallen seed becomes a tree.
In understanding this mystery, with us you'll fall.
7. Shams-i Tabrīz[2], the sun-of-truth, tells the heart, a bud yet
[to bloom,
«When your eyes open, with us, you will see...»

۳- [۹۴] - زهی عشق زهی عشق که ما راست خدایا

۱. رهی عشق زهی عشق که ما راست خدایا
چه نغز است وچه خوبست چه زیباست خدایا

۲. از آن آب حیات است که ما چرخ زنانیم
نه از کف و نه از نای نه دف هاست خدایا

۳. به هر مغز و دماغی که در افتاد خیالش
چه مغز است وچه نغز است وچه بیناست خدایا

۴. ز عکس رخ آن یار درین گلشن و گلزار
به هرسو مه و خورشید و ثریاست خدایا

۵. پر سیلیم چو جوییم همه سوی تو پوییم
که منزلگه هر سیل به دریاست خدایا

۶. بسی خوردم سوکند که خاموش کنم لیک
مگر هر دُر دریای تو کویاست خدایا

۷. ز شمس الحق تبریز دل و جان و دو دیده
سراسیمه و آشفتهٔ سوداست خدایا

III = [94] - *SO MUCH LOVE*

❧

1. So much love, we have so much love, O God.
   So beautiful, so good, so pure
2. It is this water of life that makes us turn
   not the clapping, not the music, not the sound of *daf*[1] and *nāy*[2].
3. When His fancy comes to one's mind,
   what a pearl, what a marvel, how illuminated is that mind.
4. The reflection of the beloved's face, in this flowery meadow,
   creates suns and moons and the Pleiades in every direction.
5. We are like rivers and streams, we all flow to you.
   Because at the end, all waters end in the sea, O God.
6. I swore so many times to be silent, but
   perhaps all the pearls of your sea are loquacious, O God
7. Shams-i Tabrīz makes my heart, my soul and my two eyes,
   dumbstruck and stupefied from passion, O God.

۴- [۱۲۸] - ما را سفری فتاد بی ما

۱. ما را سفری فتاد بی ما
   آنجا دل ما گشاد بی ما

۲. آن مه که ز ما نهان همی شد
   رخ بر رخ ما نهاد بی ما

۳. چون در غم دوست جان بدادیم
   ما را غم او بزاد بی ما

۴. ماییم همیشه مست بی می
   ماییم همیشه شاد بی ما

۵. ما را مکنید یاد هرگز
   ما خود هستیم یاد بی ما

۶. بی ما شده ایم شاد گوییم
   ای ما که همیشه باد بی ما

۷. در ها همه بسته بود بر ما
   بگشود چو راه داد بی ما

۸. ماییم ز نیک و بد رهیده
   از طاعت و از فساد بی ما

IV = [128] - *DEVOID OF SELF*

1. *D*EVOID of self I traveled to a place.
   There, in the absence of I, joy filled my heart.

2. Without I, His obscured face, like the moon
   came forth and kissed my cheek.

3. In longing for my love I perished
   and from that longing, birth was given to me.

4. I am eternally drunk, without wine.
   My joy is endless, without I.

5. Do not remember me, ever.
   For I am memory itself, without I.

6. I am ecstatic without myself, so I say,
   «O me, may you always be without I.»

7. All the doors were shut to me, and
   all opened when He let me in, without I.

8. Me, I am the one, free of good and evil,
   free from obedience and corruption, without I.

۵-[۱۳۲] - **در میان پردهٔ خون عشق را گلزارها**

۱. در میان پردهٔ خون عشق را گلزارها
عاشقان را با جمال عشق بی چون کارها

۲. عقل گوید: «شش جهت حدّست و بیرون راه نیست»
عشق گوید: «راه هست و رفته ام من بارها»

۳. عقل بازاری بدید و تاجری آغاز کرد
عشق دیده زان سوی بازار او بازارها

۴. ای بسا منصور پنهان ز اعتماد جان عشق
ترک منبرها بگفته بر شده بر دارها

۵. عاشقان دُرد کش را در درونه ذوق ها
عاقلان تیره دل را در درون انکارها

۶. عقل گوید: «پا منه کاندر فنا جز خار نیست»
عشق گوید عقل را: «کاندر تو است آن خارها»

۷. هین خمش کن خار هستی را ز پای دل بکن
تا ببینی در درون خویشتن گلزارها

۸. شمس تبریزی تویی خورشید اندر ابر حرف
چون برآمد آفتابت محو شد گفتارها

DĪVĀN-I SHAMS-I TABRĪZ

V = [132] - *WITHIN THE BLOODIED CAUL*

❦

1. WITHIN the bloodied caul, there are gardens of love;
Faced with the incomprehensible beauty of the beloved, lovers
[become overwhelmed.

2. Reason dictates: «There are only six ways[1] to go, and no way
[around that.»
Love says: «There are ways beyond this; many times I have
[traveled them.»

3. Reason came across a bazaar and became a merchant.
Love has seen many bazaars, and is beyond haggling.

4. Many an unknown Mansūr[2], trusting in the soul of love
has come down from the pulpit and gone up to the gallows.

5. Lovers, who drink the dregs[3], have such joy within.
The dark-hearted men of reason can only deny.

6. Reason says: «Do not enter, annihilation[4] in God has nothing
[but thorns.»
Love says to reason: «Those thorns are only in you.»

7. Be silent, pluck the thorn of existence[5] from the depths of your
[heart,
to see a myriad of rose gardens within yourself.

8. O, Shams-i Tabrīz, you are the sun, obscured by words.
When your rays break through, words will disappear.

✺

۶ - [۱۶۳] - **بروید ای حریفا   بکشید یار ما را**

۱. بروید ای حریفان بکشید یار ما را
به من آورید آخر صنم گریز پا را

۲. به ترانه های شیرین به بهانه های زرّین
بکشید سوی خانه مه خوب خوش لقا را

۳. و گر او بوعده گوید که دمی دگر بیایم
همه وعده باشد مکر بفریبد او شما را

۴. دم سخت گرم دارد که بجادویی و افسون
بزند گره بر آب او و ببندد او هوا را

۵. به مبارکی و شادی چو نگار من در آید
بنشین نظاره می کن تو عجایب خدا را

۶. چو جمال او بتابد چه بود جمال خوبان؟
که رخ چو آفتابش بکُشد چراغ ها را

۷. برو ای دل سبک رو به یَمَن به دلبر من
برسان سلام و خدمت تو عقیق بی بها را

DĪVĀN-I SHAMS-I TABRĪZ

VI = [163] - *O FRIENDS*

❦

1. *O* FRIENDS, go and drag forth my beloved.
   Bring me, at last, that adored fugitive.
2. Drag home that radiant moon,
   drag him by siren songs, and golden promises.
3. And if he promises to come later,
   know that his promise is a ruse and that he deceives you.
4. So seductive is his speech that with charm and sorcery,
   he ties knots with water and chains the air.
5. When my love comes with auspiciousness and joy,
   sit down and gaze at God's wonders.
6. His radiant face obscures all light
   and when it shines forth, what becomes of the beautiful ones?
7. Go to Yemen[1], O joyful heart, relate my loyalty to the beloved,
   and give my regards to that priceless agate.

۷-[۱۸۲] - در میان عاشقان عاقل مبا

۱. در میان عاشقان عاقل مبا
خاصه در عشق چنین شیرین لقا

۲. دور بادا عاقلان از عاشقان
دور بادا بوی گلخن از صبا

۳. گر در آید عاقلی گو: «راه نیست»
ور در آید عاشقی صد مرحبا

۴. عقل تا تدبیر و اندیشه کند
رفته باشد عشق تا هفتم سما

۵. عقل تا جوید شتر از بهر حج
رفته باشد عشق بر کوه صفا

۶. عشق آمد این دهانم را گرفت
که گذر از شعر و بر شُعرا برآ

DĪVĀN-I SHAMS-I TABRĪZ

VII ≈ [182] ~ *LET THERE BE*

⚜

1. *L*ET there be no sanity among lovers,
especially lovers of such sweetness.

2. May the men of reason stay far from the lovers.
May the stench of the furnace be far from the lovers' breeze[1].

3. If a sane man comes, tell him, «None may enter.»
If the lover comes, give a thousand welcomes.

4. By the time reason thinks to intervene
Love will have ascended to the seventh heaven.

5. By the time reason finds a camel for *hajj*[2],
Love will have scaled mount Safa[3].

6. Love came, closed my mouth and said:
«Transcend poetry and reach for the stars[4].»

❈

۸-[۱۸۹] - آمد بهار جان ها ای شاخ تر به رقص آ

۱. آمد بهار جان ها ای شاخ تر به رقص آ
چون یوسف اندر آمد مصر و شکر برقص آ

۲. چوگان زلف دیدی چون گوی در رسیدی
از پا و سر بریدی بی پا و سر برقص آ

۳. تیغی بدست خونی آمد مرا که: «چونی؟»
گفتم: «بیا که خیر است» گفتا: «نه شر، برقص آ»

۴. ای مست هست گشته بر تو فنا نوشته
رقعهٔ فنا رسیده بهر سفر به رقص ا

۵. پایان جنگ آمد آواز چنگ آمد
یوسف زچاه آمد ای بی هنر به رقص آ

۶. تا چند وعده باشد وین سر به سجده باشد؟
هجرم ببرده باشد درنگ و اثر به رقص آ

۷. کی باشد ان زمانی گوید مرا فلانی:
«کای بی خبر فنا شو ای با خبر به رقص آ»

۸. طاووس ما در آید و آن رنگ ها بر آید
با مرغ جان سراید: «بی بال و پر به رقص ا»

DĪVĀN-I SHAMS-I TABRĪZ

VIII = [189] - *SPRING IS HERE MY SOUL*

⚜

1. SPRING is here my soul[1], O budding branch, begin to dance.
Joseph[2] is here; O sugar and Egypt, begin to dance.

2. O polo ball, you saw the mallet coming and ran to it[3],
[O! that lock of hair.
You lost your head and feet, now begin to dance.

3. Bloody sword in hand[4], he came to me, saying: «How are you?»
«Come, all is calm» I said; he said «No, all is chaos. Begin to
[dance.»

4. You, drunk with existence[5], death is your destiny.
The decree of annihilation[6] is here. For the journey, begin to
[dance.

5. The end of the battle arrives, the sound of the harp begins;
Joseph is drawn from the well. O artless one, begin to dance.

6. When will you keep your promise? How long must I remain
[prostrate?
Separation has left me mute and worn[7]. Come, begin to dance.

7. The time will come when you will say: «Ignorant one!
Cease to exist[8]. You, who know, begin to dance.»

8. My peacock will appear, his colors will shine, he'll call
to the bird of the soul: «Without wings, begin to dance.»

کور و کران عالم دید از مسیح مرهم
گفته مسیح مریم: «کای کور و کر به رقص آ»

۱۰ مخدوم شمس دین است تبریز رشک چین است
اندر بهار حسنش شاخ و شجر به رقص آ

9. Jesus cured the deaf and blind; Jesus son of Mary said: «O blind and deaf, begin to dance.»

10. The Master is the sun of holiness. Tabrīz is the envy of China. In his vernal beauty, O trees and branches, begin to dance.

۹ - [۲۰۹] ای در ما را زده ما را زده شمع سرایی درآ

۱. ی در ما را زده شمع سرایی درآ
خانهٔ دل آن توست خانه خدایی درآ

۲. خانه ز تو تافته ست روشنیی یافته ست
ی دل و جان جای تو ای تو کجایی درآ

۳. ی صنم خانگی مایهٔ دیوانگی
ی همه خوبی ترا پس تو کرایی درآ

DĪVĀN-I SHAMS-I TABRĪZ

IX = [209] - *YOU WHO KNOCK AT MY DOOR*

1. You who knock at my door, enter, illuminate these dwellings.
   My heart is your home, you are the master. Enter.
2. From you this house finds brilliance and warmth.
   O you, master of my heart and soul, where are you? Enter.
3. O lord of this house, cause of my insanity,
   all goodness belongs to you. To whom do you belong? Enter.

۱۰ - [۲۳۸] - هله ای کیا نفسی بیا

۱. هله ای کیا نفسی بیا
در عیش را سره برگشا

۲. این فلان چه شد آن فلان چه شد
نبود مرا سر ماجرا

۳. نهلد کسی سر زلف او
نرهد دلی ز چنین لقا

۴. نکند کسی ز خوشی سفر
نرود کسی ز چنین سرا

۵. بهل این همه بده آن قدح
که شنیده ام کرم شما

۶. قدحی که آن پر دل شود
بپرد دلم به سوی سما

۷. خمش این نفس دم دل مزن
که فدای تو دل و جان ما

DĪVĀN-I SHAMS-I TABRĪZ

X ≈ [238] - *FOR A MOMENT*

1. *F*OR a moment, come my Lord,
   Open wide the door of life.
2. What happened to this, what happened to the other?
   I don't have a clue.
3. No one would give up a single lock of the Lover's hair.
   No heart would surrender up such beauty.
4. No one would leave behind such happiness.
   No one would abandon such a home.
5. Forget about all this, give me the cup
   as I have heard of your generosity.
6. Give me that cup which will be the wings for the heart,
   and my heart will fly to the sky above.
7. Silence, dare not speak your heart.
   Let my heart and soul be your sacrifice.

۱۱ - [۲۵۰] - هین که منم بر در در بر گشا

۱. هین که منم بر در در بر گشا
بستن در نیست نشان رضا

۲. در دل هر ذرّه ترا درگهیست
تا نگشایی بود آن در خفا

۳. فالق اصباحی و ربّ الفلق
باز کنی صد درو گویی در آ

۴. نی که منم بر در بلکه تویی
راه بده در بگشا خویش را

۵. آمد کبریت بر آتشی
گفت برون آ بر من دلبرا

۶. صورت من صورت تو نیست لیک
جمله توام صورت من چون غطا

۷. صورت و معنی تو شوم چون رسی
سو شود صورت من در لقا

۸. آتش گفتش که: «برون آمدم
ز خود خود روی بپوشم چرا؟»

۹. هین بستان از من و تبلیغ کن
بر همه اصحاب و همه اقربا

XI = [250] - *LO! I AM AT YOUR THRESHOLD*

❧

1. *L*O! I am at your threshold. Open the door...
   Keeping the door shut is no sign of contentment.

2. In the heart of every particle, there is a doorway to you.
   That door will stay hidden until you open it.

3. You who break the dawn[1], Lord of the Morning[2],
   you open a thousand doors and say: «Come in!»

4. It is not I at the door, it's you...
   Step aside to make way for yourself.

5. Sulfur went to the door of fire.
   «Come out to me, my beloved» he said.

6. «My face is not your face, but
   I am you: my face is a veil...

7. «As you appear I will be you, in form and in essence...
   encountering you, my face will vanish.»

8. «I am coming out» Fire answered,
   «for why should I hide from myself?»

9. Quick! Take these words from me and convey them
   to all, followers and friends.

۱۰ کوه اگر هست چو کاهش بکشد
داده امت من صفت کهربا

۱۱ کاه ربای من کُه می کشد
به از عدم اوردم کوه حرا؟

۱۲ در دل تو جمله منم سر به سر
سوی دل خویش بیا مرحبا

۱۳ دلبرم و دل برم ایرا که هست
جوهر دل زاده ز دریای ما

۱۴ نَقل کنم ور نکنم سایه را
سایهٔ من کی بود از من جدا؟

۱۵ لیک ز جایش ببرم تا شود
وُصلت او ظاهر وقت جلا

۱۶ تا که بداند که او فرع ماست
تا که جدا گردد او از عدا

۱۷ رو بر ساقی و شنو باقیش
نات بگوید به زبان بقا

10. You can pull mountains such as straw,
    for I have given you the attribute of amber[3].

11. This amber of mine attracts mountains.
    Did I not bring mount Hira[4] forth from nothingness?

12. Everywhere in your heart, there is only me.
    Come, welcome to your heart.

13. I am the Lover, and I steal hearts; that's the way it is.
    The pearl of the heart is born of my sea.

14. Whether or not I want to bear a shadow,
    my shadow can never be separate from me.

15. Nontheless I burn it so that on the day of glory
    he will revive and be one with me.

16. He will know that he stems from me,
    He will be separate from the enemy.

17. Go to the *sāqi*[5] to hear the rest. He will say it all
    in the language of those who behold the face of the beloved[6].

۱۲ - [۳۲۸] -   **بادست مرا زان سر اندر سر و در سبلت**

۱ - بادست مرا زان سر اندر سرو در سبلت
پر باد چرا نبود سر مست چنین دولت

۲ - هر لحظه و هر ساعت بر کوری هشیاری
صد رطل در آشامم بی ساغر و بی آلت

۳ - مرغان هوایی را بازان خدایی را
زغیب به دست آرم بی صنعت و بی حیلت

۴ - خود از کف دست من مرغان عجب رویند
می از لب من جوشد در مستی آن حالت

۵ - آن دانهٔ آدم را کز سنبل او باشد
بفروشم جنّت را بر جان نُهَم جنّت

XII = [328] - ON ACCOUNT OF YOU

1. *O*N account of you there is wind in my head and my whiskers.
   Who wouldn't be drunk with pride from such good fortune?

2. Every moment, to spite sobriety
   I drink a thousand goblets, without any cup or vessel.

3. Birds of the sky, the Godly falcons,
   I capture from thin air, without trap or craft.

4. Birds of wonder grow from the palm of my hand.
   I am exultant, wine seething from my lips.

5. I swear to the ninth heaven, I would trade paradise,
   for that seed of humanity that comes from His wisp of wheat.

۱۳ - [۳۲۹] - بیایید بیایید که گلزار دمیده ست

۱. بیایید بیایید که گلزار دمیده ست
بیایید بیایید که دلدار رسیده ست

۲. بیارید به یک بار همه جان و جهان را
به خورشید سپارید که خوش تیغ کشیده ست

۳. بر آن زشت بخندید که او ناز نماید
بر آن یار بگریید که از یار بریده ست

۴. همه شهر بشورید چو اوازه درافتاد
که دیوانه دگر بار ز زنجیر رهیده ست

۵. چه روزست و چه روزست چنین روز قیامت
مگر نامهٔ اعمال ز آفاق پریده ست؟

۶. بکوبید دُهُل ها و دگر هیچ مکویید
چه جای دل و عقل است که جان نیز رمیده ست

XIII ≈ [329] - *COME, COME*

1. COME, come, the rose garden is all in bloom.
   Come, come, the beloved is here.

2. Bring all souls who have ever lived,
   give them to the sun who shows the glint of his blade.

3. Laugh at the ugly who are vainly coquettish.
   Weep for the lover who is far from the beloved.

4. O everyone, rise up! It is proclaimed
   that the madman has broken his chains!

5. What day is this? Such a day of resurrection!
   Has the Book of Deeds[1] simply flown away?

6. Beat the drum and say no more...
   Why even think of heart or mind, when the soul itself has fled.

بار دگر آن دلبر عیّار مرا یافت

۱۴- [۳۳۰]

۱. بار دگر آن دلبر عیّار مرا یافت
سرمست همی گشت ببازار مرا یافت

۲. پنهان شدم از نرگس مخمور مرا دید
بگریختم از خانهٔ خمّار مرا یافت

۳. بگریختنم چیست کزو جان نبرد کس
پنهان شدنم چیست چو صد بار مرا یافت

۴. گفتم که: «در انبوهی شهرم کی بیابد؟»
آن کس که در انبوهی اسرار مرا یافت

۵. ای مژده که آن غمزهٔ غمّاز مرا جست
وی بخت که آن طرّهٔ طرّار مرا یافت

۶. ز گلشن خود بر سر من یار گل افشاند
وان بلبل و آن نادره تکرار مرا یافت

۷. من گم شدم از خرمن آن ماه چو کیله
مروز مه اندر بن انبار مرا یافت

۸. از خون من آثار به هر راه چکیده ست
ندر پی من بود به آثار مرا یافت

۹. چون آهو از آن شیر رمیدم به بیابان
آن شیر گهِ صید به کهسار مرا یافت

DĪVĀN-I SHAMS-I TABRĪZ

XIV = [330] - ONCE AGAIN

❦

1. ONCE again that thief of hearts, found me.
   He was drunk when in the bazaar he found me.

2. I hid from those narcissus[1] drunken eyes, but He saw me.
   I ran to the house of the tavern master, but He found me.

3. Why do I run? No one can escape from Him.
   Why do I hide since a hundred times He found me.

4. I thought to hide among the crowds of the city.
   How can I hide from the one who, in the midst of great
   [mysteries, found me?

5. Good tidings[2], that glance of the beloved sought me.
   Good fortune, that deceptive ringlet found me

6. From his own garden the beloved poured roses on my head.
   That nightingale, who has no equal found me.

7. I disappeared like the needle into the haystack of the beloved.
   Today, at the bottom of the stack, he found me[3].

8. Drops of my blood lay on all roads.
   Following the traces, He found me.

9. From that lion, like a deer on the plain, I ran.
   That lion, hunting on the mountains, found me.

۱۰ آن کس که به گردون رود و گیرد آهو
با صبر و تأنّی و به هنجار مرا یافت

۱۱ در کام من این شست و من اندر تک دریا
صاید به سر رشتهٔ جرّ ر مرا یافت

۱۲ جامی که برد از دلم آزار به من داد
آن لحظه که آن یار کم آزار مرا یافت

۱۳ این جان گران جان سبکی یافت، بپرید
کان رطل گران سنگ سبکبار مرا یافت

۱۴ مروز نه هوش است و نه گوش است و نه گفتار
کان اصل هر اندیشه و گفتار مرا یافت

✻

10. The one who rides his chariot to catch deer,
    with great patience and skill, at the end, found me.
11. I was at the bottom of the sea, with hook in my mouth.
    At the end of his line, the fisherman found me.
12. The cup He gave me freed my heart from all pain,
    at the moment that loving friend found me.
13. This heavy soul became weightless and took to flight
    when this heart of stone found that chalice of wine.
14. Today, all are stupefied, none hear and none speak,
    because the source of all thought and words found me.

۱۵-[۲۴۱] - بیا کامروز ما را روز عید است

۱. بیا کامروز ما را روز عید است
ازین پس عیش و عشرت بر مزیدست

۲. بزن دستی بگو کامروز شادیست
که روز خوش هم از اول پدید است

۳. چو یار ما در این عالم که باشد؟
چنین عیدی به صد دوران که دیده ست؟

۴. زمین و آسمان‌ها پر شکر شد
به هر سویی شکرها بر دمیده ست

۵. رسید آن بانگ موج گوهر افشان
جهان پر موج و در یا نا پدید است

۶. محمّد باز از معراج آمد
ز چارم چرخ عیسی در رسیده ست

۷. هر آن نقدی کز اینجا نیست قلب است
میی کز جام جان نبود پلید است

۸. حماری داشتم من در ارادت
ندانستم که حق ما را مرید است

۹. کنون من خفتم و پاها کشیدم
چو دانستم که بختم می کشیده ست

XV = [341] - TODAY IS THE DAY

1. *T*ODAY is the day for us to celebrate.
   From here on there will be ever increasing revelry.
2. Clap your hands, today is the day of happiness.
   A good day is apparent from the break of dawn.
3. Who in this world could possibly compare to our beloved?
   Who, in countless eons has seen such festivity?
4. The earth and heavens have become full of sweetness.
   Everywhere sugar cane has sprung forth.
5. The call of that wave brings forth the sound of pearls.
   The world is full of waves yet the sea is unseen.
6. Mohammed returns from his ascension[1].
   Jesus arrives from the fourth heaven.
7. The gold that is not from here is adulterated.
   The wine that is not from the cup of the spirit is putrid.
8. Lost in the depths of my longing for devotion to you,
   I didn't know that You longed for me.
9. Now I lay down and stretch my legs
   for my good fortune has shown its face[2].

۱۲ - [۳۹۰] - ساربانا اشتران بین اشتران بین

۱ ساربانا اشتران بین سر به سر قطار مست
سیر مست وخواجه مست و یار مست اغیار مست

۲ باغبانا رعد مطرب ابرساقی گشت و شد
باغ مست و راغ مست و غنچه مست و خار مست

۳ آسمانا چند گردی؟ گردش عنصر ببین
آب مست و باد مست و خاک مست و نار مست

۴ حال صورت این چنین و حال معنی خود بپرس
روح مست و عقل مست و وهم مست اسرار مست

۵ رو تو جباری رها کن خاک شو تا بنگری
ذرّه ذرّهٔ خاک را از خالق جبّار مست

۶ تا نگویی در زمستان باغ را مستی نماند
مدّتی پنهان شده ست از دیدهٔ مکار مست

DĪVĀN-I SHAMS-I TABRĪZ

XVI = [390] - *O LEADER OF THE CARAVAN*

❦

1. *O* LEADER of the caravan, look at your camels, the whole
[train is drunk!
The prince is drunk, the lord is drunk, friends and strangers,
[they all are drunk.

2. O Gardner, the thunder became the musician, and the clouds
[poured forth the wine
thus, did the garden become drunk, the orchard, the rosebud
[and the thorn, all are drunk.

3. O sky, how long do you turn and turn? Behold the whirling
[of the elements!
Water is drunk, Wind and Earth and Fire, all are drunk.

4. If this is the case in the world we see, just imagine the unseen
[world.
The soul is drunk, reason, imagination, and the mysteries, all
[are drunk.

5. Rid yourself of your own tyranny. Become dirt and see that
every particle of earth is drunk with the tyranny of the
[creator[1].

6. If you think that in winter the drunk is no more in the garden
know that he has been in hiding, from your guileful eye.

٧ بیخ های آن درختان می نهانی می خورند
روزکی دو صبر می کن تا شود بیدار مست

٨ گر ترا کوبی رسد از رفتن مستان مرنج
با چنان ساقی و مطرب کی رود هموار مست؟

٩ ساقیا باده یکی کن چند باشد عربده
دوستان زاقرار مست و دشمنان ز انکار مست

١٠ باده را افزون بده تا برگشاید این گره
باده تا در سر نیفتد کی دهد دستار مست؟

١١ بُخل ساقی باشد آنجا یا فساد باده ها
هر دو نا هموار باشد چون رود رهوار مست

١٢ روی های زرد بین و بادهٔ گلگون بده
زانک ازین گلگون ندارد بر رخ و رخسار مست

١٣ باده ای داری خدایی بس سبک خوار و لطیف
زان اگر خواهد بنوشد روز صد خروار مست

١٤ شمس تبریزی به دورت هیچکس هشیار نیست
کافر ومؤ من خراب و زاهد و خمّار مست

7. The roots of the trees are secretly drinking wine.
   Wait a while, when they waken, they too will be drunk.

8. If you receive a blow from a staggering drunk, don't take it hard.
   With such a cup-bearer and such a minstrel how can a drunk
   [walk straight?

9. O *sāqi*, dispense wine to all, end the uproar...
   Friends are drunk from acceptance and the enemy from denial.

10. Pour more wine, untie this knot, for if
    the wine doesn't go to your head how do you give up the turban?

11. It is either the avarice of the cup-bearer or the wine is bad.
    All is wrong if the drunk is walking straight.

12. Behold these pale faces, pour your rosy wine.
    For lack of it the cheeks of the drunkard are sallow.

13. Yours is the Divine wine, delicate and light to drink.
    Whosoever wishes can drink a thousand barrels a day.

14. O Shams-i Tabrīz, in your company none are sober.
    The infidel and the pious are intoxicated, the ascetic and the
    [vintner, all are drunk.

۱۷-[۴۴۱] - بنمای رخ که باغ و گلستانم آرزوست

۱. بنمای رخ که باغ و گلستانم آرزوست
بگشای لب که قند فراوانم آرزوست

۲. ای آفتاب حسن برون آ دمی ز ابر
کان چهرهٔ مشعشع تابانم آرزوست

۳. بشنیدم از هوای تو آواز طبل بار
بازآمدم که ساعد سلطانم آرزوست

۴. گفتی ز ناز: «بیش مرنجان مرا برو»
ن گفتنت که بیش مرنجانم آرزوست

۵. وان دفع گفتنت که: «برو شه به خانه نیست»
وان ناز و باز و تندی در بانم ارزوست

۶. یعقوب وار وا اسفاها همی زنم
دیدار خوب یوسف کنعانم آرزوست

۷. والله که شهری بی تو مرا حبس می شود
وارگی و کوه و بیابانم آرزوست

XVII ≈ [441] - *SHOW YOUR FACE*

1. *S*HOW your face, the rose garden, the flower bed. That's what
   [I long for.
   Open your lips, pour an ocean of sweetness. That's what
   [I long for.

2. O, sun of beauty! Emerge from the clouds,
   Seeing Your radiant, luminous face. That's what I long for.

3. Out of yearning for You I heard the beating of the falcon drum[1]
   I flew back to rest on the armlet of the King. That's what
   [I longed for.

4. Coyly, you said: «Bother me no more, leave!»
   The moment you say: «Bother me no more!» That's what
   [I long for.

5. When you harshly say: «Go away! The King is not home.»
   The doorkeeper's rudeness, that pride, that anger. That's what
   [I long for.

6. As Jacob I cry: «Alas, alas» in my mourning.
   The lovely countenance of Joseph of Canaan. That's what
   [I long for.

7. Without you, I swear by God, this city is a prison to me.
   Wandering in the wilderness and amongst the mountains. That's
   [what I long for.

۱. زین همرهان سست عناصر دلم گرفت
شیرخدا و رستم دستانم آرزوست

۲. جانم ملول گشت ز فرعون و ظلم او
ن نور روی موسی عمرانم آرزوست

۳. زین خلق پر شکایت گریان شدم ملول
ن های و هوی و نعرهٔ مستانم آرزوست

۴. گویا ترم ز بلبل امّا ز رشک عام
مُهرست بر دهانم و افغانم آرزوست

۵. دی شیخ با چراغ همی گشت گرد شهر
کز دیو و دَد ملولم و انسانم آرزوست

۶. گفتند: «یافت می نشود جسته ایم ما»
گفت: «آن که یافت می نشود آنم آرزوست»

۷. پنهان ز دیدها و همه دیدها ازوست
ن آشکار صنعت پنهانم آرزوست

۷. گوشم شنید قصهٔ ایمان و مست شد
کوقسم چشم؟ صورت ایمانم آرزوست

۷. یک دست جام باده و یک دست جعد یار
رقصی چنین میانهٔ میدانم آرزوست

۷. بنمای شمس مفخر تبریز رو ز شرق
من هدهدم حضور سلیمانم آرزوست

8. Of my fainthearted fellow travelers, my heart grows heavy.
   The Lion of God[2] and Rostam[3], son of Dastan. That's what
   [I long for.

9. My soul is oppressed by Pharaoh and his tyranny.
   The face of Moses and the light radiating from it. That's what
   [I long for.

10. Of those, so full of lament and constant weeping I grow weary.
    The clamor, howling and shouts of the drunk. That's what
    [I long for.

11. I am more eloquent than a nightingale, yet for people's envy,
    I have a seal on my lips, but to cry out. That's what I long for.

12. Yesterday, the *shaikh*, with a lamp searched around the town.
    He said: «Of wild beasts and demons I grow weary. I long to find
    [human beings.»

13. They said: «We have looked, and found none.»
    He said: «That which has not been found, that's what I long for.»

14. He is hidden from all eyes, yet all eyes come from Him.
    That hidden One whose art is apparent; He is the one I long for.

15. My ear heard the voice of Faith and grew intoxicated.
    Where is the lot of the eye? The face of the Faith. That's what
    [I long for.

16. In one hand a cup of wine, in the other a lock of the Beloved's
    [hair;
    to dance such a dance in the middle of the square, that's what
    [I long for.

17. Show your face from the East O, Shams, pride of Tabrīz.
    I am the hoopoe[4], the presence of Solomon, that's what I long for.

۱۸ - [۵۷۴] - مرا عاشق چنان باید که هر باری که بر خیزد

۱ مرا عاشق چنان باید که هر باری که بر خیزد
   قیامت های پر آتش ز هر سویی برانگیزد

۲ دلی خواهیم چون دوزخ که دوزخ را فرو سوزد
   دو صد دریا بشوراند ز موج بحر نگریزد

۳ فلک هار اچو مندیلی به دست خویش در پیچد
   چراغ لا یزالی را چو قندیلی در آویزد

۴ چو شیری سوی جنگ آید دل او چون نهنگ آید
   به جز خود هیچ نگذارد و با خود نیز بستیزد

۵ چو هفتصد پردهٔ دل را به نور خود بدرّاند
   ز عرشش این ندا آید: «بنامیزد بنامیزد»

۶ چو او از هفتمین دریا به کوه قاف رو آرد
   از آن دریا چه گوهر ها کنار خاک در ریزد

XVIII ≈ [574] - *FOR ME A LOVER IS SUCH*

1. *F*OR me a lover is such that each time he rises,
an ethereal fiery storm surrounds him.
2. With the flame in his heart he burns out the fires of Hell.
A heart, which creates tumult in a hundred seas and doesn't
[flee from the waves.
3. He wraps the heavens around his hand like a handkerchief,
and hangs the eternal light like a lantern.
4. Like a lion he faces the battlefield, with a heart as great as a whale.
Nothing must be left standing around him. Not even he escapes
[unassailed.
5. When his light tears through the seven hundred veils of the heart,
from the throne of God he will hear cheers of bravo! Bravo!
6. When he sets out from the seventh sea for mount Qāf[1],
what pearls will spill forth from that sea onto the dusty shores.

۱۹ - [۵۹۵] - آن را که درون دل عشق و طلبی باشد

۱ ن را که درون دل عشق و طلبی باشد
چون دل نگشاید در آن را سببی باشد

۲ رو بر در دل بنشین کان دلبر پنهانی
وقت سحری آید یا نیمشبی باشد

۳ جانی که جدا گردد جویای خدا گردد
او نادره ای باشد او بوالعجبی باشد

۴ ن دیده کزین ایوان ایوان دگر بیند
صاحب نظری باشد شیرین لقبی باشد

۵ ن کس که چنین باشد با روح قرین باشد
در ساعت جان دادن او را طربی باشد

۶ پایش چو به سنگ آید دُرَیش به چنگ آید
جانش چو به لب آید با قند لبی باشد

۷ چون تاج ملوکانش در چشم نمی‌آید
او بی پدر و مادر عالی نسبی باشد

۸ خاموش کن و هر جا اسرار مکن پیدا
در جمع سبکِ روحان هم بولَهَبی باشد

DĪVĀN-I SHAMS-I TABRĪZ

XIX = [595] - *WHEN YOU HAVE LOVE*

⚜

1. WHEN you have love and yearning in your heart, but the door doesn't open, know there is a reason!
2. Go, sit at the heart's doorstep, and in the midst of the night, or perhaps at dawn's wakening the secret beloved will appear.
3. A rare and wondrous thing is a soul, detached from the world, seeking God.
4. Eyes that see from this world to the next belong to the clear sighted and possess a gifted status.
5. He who owns this vision is one with the Spirit. He rejoices at the moment of death.
6. Tripping on a stone he finds a pearl. His soul leaves his lips to kiss lips sweeter.
7. Since the crown of a King is nothing in his eyes, although low borne, he embodies nobility.
8. Silence! Don't reveal secrets just anywhere: even in the assembly of pure souls, there is a Abū Lahab[1].

۲۰ - [۶۲۲] - جان پیش تو هر ساعت می ریزد و می روید

۱ - جان پیش تو هر ساعت می ریزد و می روید
از بهر یکی جان کس چون با تو سخن گوید؟

۲ - هر جا که نهی پایی از خاک بروید سر
وز بهر یکی سر کس دست از تو کجا شوید؟

۳ - روزی که بپرد جان از لذت بوی نو
جان داند و جان داند کز دوست چه می بوید

۴ - یک دم که خمار تو از مغز شود کم تر
صد نوحه بر ارد سر هر موی همی موید

۵ - من خانه تهی کردم کز رخت تو پُردارم
می کاهم تا عشقت افزاید و افزوید

۶ - جانم ز پی عشق شمس الحق تبریزی
بی پای چو کشتی ها در بحر همی پوید

XX ≈ [622] - *How Can One*

1. *H*OW can one argue for the value of this life,
   when every moment, I die at your feet and am revived?
2. Wherever your foot falls, a new head springs forth from the [earth.
   How does one give you up for the sake of one's own unworthy [head?
3. The day the soul flies in the rapture of your scent
   The soul and only the soul will know the fragrance of the friend.
4. If for a moment this infatuation with you leaves me,
   my head will sing a thousand laments, every hair will moan.
5. I emptied my house to have it filled with your goods.
   I make room for the sake of your ever increasing love.
6. In the search for the love of Shams-i Tabrīz, my soul
   without feet will walk the seas like ships.

۲۱ - [۶۴۸] - ای قوم به حج رفته کجایید کجایید؟

۱ ای قوم به حج رفته کجایید کجایید؟
معشوق همین جاست بیایید بیایید

۲ معشوق تو همسایهٔ دیوار به دیوار
در بادیه سر گشته شما در چه هوایید؟

۳ گر صورت بی صورت معشوق ببینید
هم خواجه و هم خانه و هم کعبه شمایید

۴ ده بار از آن راه بدان خانه برفتید
یک بار ازین خانه براین بام برآیید

۵ آن خانه لطیف است نشان هاش بگفتید
از خواجهٔ آن خانه نشانی بنمایید

۶ یک دستهٔ گل کو اگر آن باغ بدیدیت
یک گوهر جان کو اگر از بحر خدایید

۷ با این همه آن رنج شما گنج شما باد
افسوس که بر گنج شما پرده شمایید

XXI = [648] - O You, Who have Gone

1. O you, who have gone to *hajj*[1], where are you? Where are you?
   The beloved is right here. Come, come.
2. Your beloved shares the same wall with you.
   What are you looking for – stranded – in the desert?
3. If you see the faceless face of the beloved,
   you'll know you are the lord, the house and the Ka'ba[2].
4. Ten times you traveled the road, to that house.
   Climb up once, from this house to the roof.
5. That house is beautiful; you described it point by point.
   Give me a sign from the lord of that house.
6. Where are the roses you picked if you saw that garden?
   Where is just one pearl of the soul if you are from the sea of God.
7. Whatever is your toil is also your treasure.
   Alas, the veil that covers your own treasure is you.

۲۲ - [۶۴۹] - بر چرخ سحرگاه یکی ماه عیان شد

۱. برچرخ سحرگاه یکی ماه عیان شد
از چرخ فرود آمد و در ما نگران شد

۲. چون باز که برباید مرغی به گهِ صید
بربود مرا آن مه و بر چرخ روان شد

۳. درخود چو نظر کردم خود را بندیدم
زیرا که در آن مه تنم از لطف چو جان شد

۴. در جان چو سفر کردم جز ماه ندیدم
تا سرِّ تجلّیِ ازل جمله بیان شد

۵. نه چرخ فلک جمله دران ماه فرو شد
کشتی وجودم همه در بحر نهان شد

۶. ن بحر بزد موج و خرد باز بر آمد
وآوازه در افکند چنین گشت و چنان شد

۷. ن بحر کفی کرد و به هر پاره از آن کف
نقشی ز فلان آمد و جسمی ز فلان شد

۸. هر پاره کف جسم کزان بحر نشان یافت
در حال گدازید و در آن بحر روان شد

۹. بی دولت مخدومی شمس الحق تبریز
نی ماه توان دیدن ونی بحر توان شد

XXII = [649] - AT DAWN

1. At dawn, a moon appeared on the wheel of heaven.
   Descending from the wheel it gazed at me.

2. Like the falcon, which snatches a bird, when hunting,
   that moon snatched me up and ran to the wheel.

3. When I looked at myself, I could not see me,
   for in that moon my body had become so gossamer, it seemed
   [a spirit.

4. When I traveled in the Spirit, I saw nothing but the moon,
   until all the secrets of the time before creation were told.

5. All nine heavens sunk into the moon.
   The ship of my existence was swallowed by the sea.

6. Reason re-surfaced in the waves of the sea,
   and began to boast of all it had seen.

7. That sea fermented and from each foamy wave,
   images and bodies of men and women appeared.

8. Each body that was brought to life by the foaming of the sea,
   then and there melted and flowed back into the sea.

9. Without the good fortune of being the servant of Shams-i Tabrīz,
   one can neither see the moon nor become the sea.

۲۳ - [۶۵۰] - آن سرخ قبایی که چو مه پار بر آمد

۱   ن سرخ قبایی که چو مه پار بر آمد
    امسال در این خرقهٔ زنگار بر آمد

۲   ن ترک که آن سال به یغماش بدیدی
    ن است که امسال عرب وار بر آمد

۳   ن یار همانست اگر جامه دگر شد
    ن جامه بَدَل کرد و دگر بار بر آمد

۴   ن باده همانست اگر شیشه بَدَل شد
    بنگر که چه خوش بر سر خمّار بر آمد

۵   شب رفت حریفان صبوحی به کجایید
    کان مشعله از روزن اسرار بر آمد

۶   رومی پنهان گشت چو دوران حبش دید
    امروز در این لشکر جرّار بر آمد

۷   شمس الحق تبریز رسیده ست بگویید
    کز چرخ صفا آن مه انوار بر آمد

XXIII = [650] - *THE ONE WHO APPEARED*

1. THE one who appeared like a moon, in a crimson cloak, last year,
   this year he came in a brown robe.
2. The Turk you saw plundering that year,
   is the same one who appeared as an Arab this year.
3. Even though the garment is changed, the beloved is the same.
   He changed the garment and reappeared.
4. The wine is the same, although the jug is changed.
   See how beautifully it goes to the head of the drunk.
5. From the window of secrets that torch came in, night passes,
   O companions of the cup of dawn, where are you?
6. The Roman hid when he saw the Abyssinian's time had come.
   And today he is part of this glorious army.
7. Proclaim that Tabrīz's sun of truth is here.
   That moon of light came from the heaven of purity.

۲۴-[۶۸۳] - ز خاک من اگر گندم بر آید

۱. ز خاک من اگر گندم بر آید
از آن گر نان پزی مستی فزاید

۲. خمیر و نانبا دیوانه گردد
تنورش بیت مستانه سراید

۳. اگر بر گور من ایی زیارت
ترا خرپشته ام رقصان نماید

۴. میا بی دف به گور من برادر
که در بزم خدا غمگین نشاید

۵. زنخ بر بسته و در گور خفته
دهان افیون و نقل یار خاید

۶. بدری زان کفن بر سینه بندی
خراباتی ز جانت در گشاید

۷. ز هر سو بانک چنگ و چنگ مستان
ز هر کاری بلابدُ کار زاید

۸. مرا حق از می عشق افریده ست
همان عشقم اگر مرگم بساید

۹. منم مستی و اصل من می عشق
بگو از می به جز مستی چه آید

۱۰. به برج روح شمس الدین تبریز
بپرد روح من یک دم نپاید

DĪVĀN-I SHAMS-I TABRĪZ

XXIV ≈ [683] - *IF YOU BAKE BREAD*

❖

1. *I*F you bake bread from the wheat
   that grows on my grave, it will intoxicate.
2. The baker and the dough, both will go crazy.
   The oven will compose euphoric verse.
3. If you come to visit my grave,
   you'll see my tombstone dancing.
4. But don't come to my grave without a *daf*¹, brother
   for at the feast of God there is no sorrow.
5. Deep in the grave, with my chin tied closed,
   my mouth is full of sweets and opium.
6. If you tear a piece of my shroud and wear it on your chest
   an entire tavern² opens from within you.
7. Drunks all around, shouting, fighting and playing the harp:
   everything, must give birth to something else.
8. God has made me of love's wine.
   Even as death consumes me I am that love.
9. I am drunkenness originating from that wine of love.
   Tell me, what can wine bring but euphoria?
10. My soul cannot wait to fly
    to the high tower, that is the spirit of Shams-i Tabrīz.

۲۰ - [۶۸۶] - ای مطرب جان چو دف به دست آمد

۱. ای مطرب جان چو دف به دست آمد
  این پرده بزن که یار مست آمد

۲. چون چهره نمود آن بت زیبا
  ماه از سوی چرخ بت پرست آمد

۳. درّات جهان به عشق آن خورشید
  رقصان ز عدم به سوی هست آمد

۴. غمگین ز چه ای مکر ترا غولی
  از راه ببرد و هم نشست آمد؟

۵. ران غول ببر بگیر سغراقی
  کان بر کف عشق از الست آمد

۶. این پرده بزن که مشتری از چرخ
  از بهر شکستگان به پست آمد

۷. در حلقهٔ این شکستگان گردید
  کان دولت و بخت در شکست آمد

۸. این عشرت و عیش چون نماز آمد
  وین دُردی دَرد اَبدست آمد

۹. خامش کن و در خمش تماشا کن
  بلبل از گفت پای بست آمد

DĪVĀN-I SHAMS-I TABRĪZ

XXV ≈ [686] - *O, Minstrel of the Soul*

❖

1. *O*, minstrel of the soul, since you have the *daf*[1] in your hand,
   Play the rhythm that emanates from the drunken state of
   [the Beloved.
2. Since the face of that beautiful one appeared,
   the heavenly moon, became an idol worshiper.
3. For love of that sun the particles of the universe
   danced forth, from nothingness into existence.
4. Why grieve? Perhaps a Demon
   became your Companion and led you astray from the path?
5. Part ways with that Demon and take hold of a jug.
   For, that jug has been in the hands of love since the dawn of time.
6. Play this tune, as for the sake of the broken ones,
   Jupiter has descended from the Heavens.
7. He danced in the circle of the broken ones,
   for he had lost all his glory and fortune.
8. This feasting and celebration became our prayer.
   These dregs of pain became our ablution.
9. Be silent and in silence watch the world.
   The nightingale is in the cage because he sang.

٢٦ - [٨٧٤] امروز مرده بین که چه سان زنده می شود

۱ - امروز مرده بین که چه سان زنده می شود
آزاد سرو بین که چه سان بنده می شود

۲ - پوسیده استخوان و کفن های مرده بین
کز روح و علم و عشق چه آکنده می شود

۳ - آن حلق و آن دهان که دریده ست در لحد
چون عندلیب مست چه گوینده می شود

۴ - آن جان به شیشه ای که ز سوزن همی گریخت
جان را به تیغ عشق فروشنده می شود

۵ - امروز کعبه بین که روان شد به سوی حاج
کز وی هزار قافله فرخنده می شود

۶ - امروز غوره بین که شکر بست از نشاط
امروز شوره بین که چه روینده می شود

۷ - می خند ای زمین که بزادی خلیفه ای
کز وی کلوخ و سنگ تو جنبنده می شود

۸ - غم مرد و گریه رفت بقای من و تو باد
هر جا که گریه ایست کنون خنده می شود

۹ - آن گلشنی شکفت که از فرّ بوی او
بی داس و تیشه خار تو بر کنده می شود

۱۰ - پاینده عمر باد روان لطیف ما
جان را بقاست تن چو قباژنده میشود

XXVI = [874] - *LOOK HOW THE DEAD*

1. *L*OOK how the dead become alive, today.
   Look how the free become enslaved, today.
2. Look at the rotten bones and the shrouds of the dead.
   Look how they become filled with soul, knowledge and love.
3. Look at that throat and mouth, torn wide in the tomb.
   Look how they sing like a drunken nightingale.
4. That tormented one who ran at the drop of a needle,
   look how he submits his soul to the sword of love[1].
5. Look at the Ka'ba[2] walking towards the pilgrims today,
   and making a thousand caravans joyful.
6. Look at the sour grape that became sweet from joy today.
   Look how the salt-marsh becomes fertile land today.
7. Laugh O earth for you gave birth to an Emperor,
   who will give life to your clods and rocks.
8. Sorrow died and weeping fled. Eternal life to you and I.
   Where there was weeping, now there will be laughter.
9. Such a garden of roses blossomed, that by the glory of its
   [perfume,
   your brambles will be hacked away without sickle and axe.
10. Let our fragile spirit have eternal life.
    The soul lives, while the body becomes worn out like a cloak.

۲۷ - [۹۱۱] - به روز مرگ چو تابوت من روان باشد

۱ به روز مرگ چو تابوت من روان باشد
گمان مبر که مرا درد این جهان باشد

۲ برای من مگری و مگو دریغ دریغ
به دوغ دیو درافتی دریغ ان باشد

۳ جنازه ام چو ببینی مگو فراق فراق
مرا وصال و ملاقات آن زمان باشد

۴ مرا به گورسپاری مگو وداع وداع
که گور پردهٔ جمعیت جنان باشد

۵ فرو شدن چو بدیدی برآمدن بنگر
غروب شمس و قمر را چرا زیان باشد؟

۶ ترا غروب نماید ولی شروق بود
لحد چو حبس نماید خلاص جان باشد

۷ کدام دانه فرورفت در زمین که نرست؟
چرا به دانهٔ انسانت این گمان باشد؟

۸ کدام دلو فرو رفت و پر برون نامد
ز چاه یوسف جان را چرا فغان باشد؟

۸ دهان چو بستی ازین سوی آن طرف بگشا
که های و هوی تو در جوّ لا مکان باشد

DĪVĀN-I SHAMS-I TABRĪZ

XXVII = [911] - ON THE DAY OF MY DEATH

❦

1. *O*N the day of my death, when my coffin passes by
do not think that my heart aches for this world.

2. Do not weep for me and don't say: «Alas, alas.»
If you fall in the trap of the Demon's deceit, that calls for alas.

3. When you see my corpse, do not say: «Separation, separation;»
for me, that will be the time of gathering and union.

4. When you entrust me to the grave, do not say: «Farewell, farewell.»
Because, the grave is the last veil to the tranquility of heaven.

5. When you see me going down, see me rising.
There is no loss in the setting of the moon and the sun.

6. It appears like sunset to you, but it is sunrise.
The grave appears like prison, but it is freedom for the soul.

7. What seed went in the ground that did not grow?
Why do you think otherwise about the seed of Man?

8. What bucket went down into the well that did not come up, full?
Why should Joseph complain of being in the well?

9. When your mouth is closed, on this side, open it on the other [side.

Because you will sing and revel in infinity.

✺

۲۸ - [۱،۰۹۵] - داد جاروبی به دستم آن نگار

۱   داد جاروبی به دستم آن نگار
    گفت: «کز دریا بر انگیزان غبار»

۲   باز آن جاروب را ز آتش بسوخت
    گفت: «کز آتش تو جارویی برآر»

۳   کردم از حیرت سجودی پیش او
    گفت: «بی ساجد سجودی خوش بیار»

۴   آه بی ساجد سجودی چون بُوَد؟
    گفت: «بی چون باشد و بی خارخار»

۵   گردنک را پیش کردم گفتمش.
    «ساجدی را سر ببر از ذوالفقار»

۶   تیغ تا او بیش زد سر بیش شد
    تا برُست ازگردنم سرصد هزار

۷   من چراغ و هرسرم همچون فتیل
    هر طرف اندر گرفته از شرار

۸   شمع ها می وَرشُد از سرهای من
    شرق تا مغرب گرفته از قطار

۹   شرق و مغرب چیست اندر لامکان؟
    گلخنی تاریک و حمامی به کار

XXVIII = [1095] - *My Love Put a Broom in my Hand*

❦

1. *M*Y love put a broom in my hand
   and said: «Stir up dust from the sea.»
2. Then He set fire to the broom and burned it.
   Then He said: «Now make a broom from fire.»
3. Out of awe I prostrated myself in front of Him.
   He said: «Prostrate yourself without the prostrator.»
4. Alas! How could there be a prostration without a prostrator?
   He said: «It would be a prostration unparalleled and delightful.»
5. I presented my neck, saying:
   «Severe the head of the prostrator with the Zulfaqār[1].»
6. The more He struck with the sword the more heads grew,
   until a hundred thousand heads grew from my neck.
7. I was a lamp and each of my heads like a wick,
   there were flames in all directions.
8. Countless candles grew from my heads.
   From East to West there were rows and rows.
9. What is East and West in the place of no place?
   A dark furnace and a warm bathhouse.

۱۰	ای مزاجت سرد، کو تاسهٔ دلت؟ اندرین گرمابه تا کی این قرار؟
۱۱	برشو از گرمابه و گلخن سرو جامه کن در بنگر آن نقش و نگار
۱۲	تا ببینی نقش های دلربا تا ببینی رنگ های لاله زار
۱۳	چون بدیدی سوی روزن در نگر کان نگار از عکس روزن شد نگار
۱۴	شش جهت حمّام و روزن لامکان برسر روزن جمال شهریار
۱۵	خاک و اب از عکس او رنگین شده جان بباریده به ترک و زنگبار
۱۶	روز رفت و قصّه ام کوته نشد ای شب و روز از حدیثش شرمسار
۱۷	شاه شمس الدین تبریزی مرا سست می دارد خمار اندر خمار

※

10. O cold blooded one, where is the agitaion of your heart?
    How long will you sit at ease in this bathhouse?

11. Ascend from the bathhouse, and don't go to the furnace.
    Clothe² yourself, look at those images and colors.

12. Until you see captivating pictures,
    until you see the colors of the flowerbed.

13. After you've seen all that, look through the opening³,
    because those pictures reflect through the opening.

14. The six directions are the bathhouse and the opening is the
    [place of no place⁴.
    Above the opening there is the beautiful face of the King.

15. The earth and water have been colored by His reflection.
    He showers life and soul from Turkey to Zanzibar.

16. The day is gone and my story has no end.
    Night and day cannot contain His story.

17. The King, Shams-i Tabrīz,
    keeps me intoxicated. Intoxication upon intoxication.

۲۹ - [۱۱۸۰] - چنان مستم چنان مستم من امروز

۱   چنان مستم چنان مستم من امروز
    که از چنبر برون جستم من امروز

۲   چنان چیزی که در خاطر نیاید
    چنانستم چنانستم من امروز

۳   به جان با آسمان عشق رفتم
    به صورت گردرین پستم من امروز

۴   گرفتم گوش عقل و گفتم: «ای عقل،
    برون رو کز تو وارستم من امروز

۵   بشوی ای عقل دست خویش از من
    که در مجنون بپیوستم من امروز»

۶   به دستم داد آن یوسف ترنجی
    که هردودست خود خستم من امروز

۷   چنانم کرد آن ابریق پُر می
    که چندین خُنب بشکستم من امروز

۸   نمی دانم کجایم لیک فرُخ
    مقامی کاندروهستم من امروز

۹   بیامد بر درم اقبال نازان
    زمستی دربراو بستم من امروز

۱۰ چو وا گشت او پی او می دویدم
    دمی از پای ننشستم من امروز

XXIX ≈ [1185] - *I AM SO DRUNK*

❦

1. *I* AM so drunk, so drunk today,
   that I jumped out of the cage, today.
2. I am in a state which cannot be imagined.
   That's how I am today.
3. With my soul, I reached to the heavens of love,
   even though my body is still in this pit, today.
4. I twisted reason's ear and said: «O reason,
   get out, I am free of you, today.»
5. O reason, wash your hands of me,
   for I have joined with Majnūn[1], today.
6. Such an orange did Joseph[2] put in my hand
   that I wounded both my hands, today.
7. I got so drunk from that flagon,
   that I broke many a jar, today.
8. I don't know where I am, today.
   But wherever I am... O what a place.
9. Good fortune came, alluringly, to my door.
   Out of drunkenness I shut the door in his face, today.
10. When he left I ran after him.
    I did not stop running for a moment, today.

۱۰ چو «نحن اقربم» معلوم آمد
دگر خود را بنپرستم من امروز

۱۲ مبند آن زلف شمس الدین تبریز
که چون ماهی درین شستم من امروز

11 Since I realized «we are closer...»[3]
   I no longer worship myself, today.

12 Don't tie back that free flowing lock of hair,
   for I am in your hand like a flopping fish, today.

۳۰. [۱۲٥٤] - من تو ام تو منی ای دوست مرو از بر خویش

۱ من ‌ توام تو منی ای دوست مرواز برخویش
خویش را غیر مینگار و مران از در خویش

۲ آن که چون سایه ز شخص تو جدا نیست منم
مکش ای دوست تو برسایهٔ خود خنجر خویش

۳ ای درختی که به هر سوت هزاران سایه ست
سایه ها را بنواز و مبُر از گوهر خویش

٤ سایه ها را همه پنهان کن و فانی درنور
بر گشا طلعت خورشیدرخ انور خویش

٥ مُلکِ دل از دو دلی تو مُخَبَّط گشته ست
بر سرتخت برآ پا مکش از منبر خویش

٦ عقل تاج است چنین گفت به تمثیل علی
تاج را گوهرنو بخش تو از گوهر خویش

XXX = [1254] - *I AM YOU, YOU ARE I*

1. *I* AM you, you are I. O beloved, don't leave yourself.
   Do not fancy yourself a stranger and don't cast him away from
   [your threshold.

2. The one who, like a shadow is inseparable from you, is me.
   Do not draw your dagger on your own shadow, friend.

3. You are a tree casting your shade in all directions.
   Be kind to your shade, don't cut it from your essence.

4. Unveil your sun-like, illuminated face
   and dissipate all the shadows, in your brilliance.

5. The realm of the heart is disturbed because of your
   [indecisiveness.
   Stay on your throne. Don't leave the pulpit.

6. «Wisdom is a crown», this is what 'Alī said symbolically.
   From your essence[1], give new gems to the crown.

۳۱-[۱۳۱۱] - باز از آن کوه قاف آمد عنقای عشق

۱ - باز از ان کوه قاف امد عنقای عشق
باز برآمد زجان نعره و هیهای عشق

۲ - باز برآورد عشق سر به مثال نهنگ
تا شکند زورق عقل به دریای عشق

۳ - ینه گشاده ست فقر جانب دل های پاک
در شکم طور بین سینهٔ سینای عشق

۴ - سرغ دل عاشقان باز پر نو گشاد
کزقفس سینه یافت عالم پهنای عشق

۵ - هر نفس آید نثار برسر یاران کار
ازبر جانان که اوست جان ودل افزای عشق

۶ - فتنه نشان عقل بود رفت وبه یک سونشست
هر طرف اکنون ببین فتنه و دروای عشق

۷ - عقل بدید آتشی گفت که: «عشق است ونی»
عشق ببیند مگر دیدهٔ بینای عشق

۸ - عشق ندای بلند کرد به اواز پست
کای دل بالا بپر بنگر بالای عشق

۹ - بنگر در شمس دین خسرو تبریزیان
شادی جان های پاک دیدهٔ دل های عشق

XXXI = [1311] - ONCE AGAIN

1. Once again, the *Anqā*[1] of love came back from mount Qāf[2].
   Once again, the roar and clamor of love rose from the soul.

2. Again like a whale, love surfaced
   to shatter the boat of reason, in the sea of love.

3. Poverty has open arms for the pure of heart.
   Look into the depths of mount Sinai[3] to see the soul of love.

4. Once again, the heart bird of the lovers spread new wings,
   since the breadth of love in the world comes from within the
   [cage of the self.

5. With each breath, grace is bestowed upon the companions of
   [the way.
   From the beloved it comes, for He is the soul, the dispenser
   [of love.

6. Reason was quashing sedition, but he went and sat at the wayside.
   Now look all around, the proud sedition of love.

7. Reason saw a fire, he said: «This is love and you are the reed.»
   Only the all seeing eye of love can see Love.

8. Love, loudly echoed its gentle call,
   saying: «O heart, fly high, look at the stature of love.»

9. Look into the holy sun – Shamseddīn – King of Tabrīz;
   the rapture of the pure souls and the vision of the lover's heart.

۳۲ - [۱۳۲۶] - عاشقی و آنگهانی نام و ننگ؟

۱ عاشقی و آنگهانی نام و ننگ؟
   اونشاید عشق را ده سنگ سنگ

۲ گر ز هر چیزی بلنگی دور شو
   راه دورو سنگلاخ و لنگ لنگ؟

۳ مرگ اگر مرد است آید پیش من
   تا کشم خود در کنارش تنگ تنگ

۴ من ازو جانی برم بی رنگ و بو
   او زمن دلقی ستاند رنگ رنگ

۵ جور و ظلم دوست را بر جان بنه
   ور نخواهی پس صلای جنگ جنگ

۶ گر نمی خواهی تراش صیقلش
   باش چون آیینهٔ پُر زنگ زنگ

۷ دست را بر چشم خود نه گو به چشم

XXXII = [1326] - *FALLING IN LOVE*

❖

1. FALLING in love and then thinking of your good name?
   You are not worthy of love and should be stoned.
2. If something makes you lame, leave it.
   A long road, full of stones and walking lame?
3. If death dares, let him come to me,
   and I will give him a tight embrace.
4. From him, I will get a pure soul,
   and from me, he will get a patched, colorful cloak[1].
5. Gladly accept the tyranny of the beloved.
   Or refuse it, and declare war.
6. If you don't want the hardship that comes with His polishing,
   then stay like an all rusted mirror[2].
7. Put your hand on your eye and bow down in obedience.
   Open your eyes, do not gaze without seeing.

۳۳ - [۱۳۹۰] - باز آمدم باز آمدم از پیش آن یار آمدم

۱   باز آمدم باز آمدم از پیش آن یار آمدم
در من نگر در من نگر بهر تو غم خوار آمدم

۲   شاد آمدم شاد آمدم از جمله آزاد آمدم
چندین هزاران سال شد تا من به گفتار آمدم

۳   آن جا روم آن جا روم بالا بدم بالا روم
بازم رهان بازم رهان کاین جا به زنهار آمدم

۴   من مرغ لاهوتی بدم دیدی که ناسوتی شدم
دامش ندیدم ناگهان در وی گرفتار آمدم

۵   من نور پاکم ای پسر نه مشت خاکم مختصر
آخر صدف من نیستم من دُرّ شهوار آمدم

۶   ما را به چشم سَر مبین مارا به چشم سِر ببین
آن جا بیا ما را ببین کاینجا سبکبار آمدم

۷   از چار مادر برترم وز هفت آبا نیز هم
من گوهر کانی بُدم کاینجا به دیدار آمدم

۸   یارم ببازار آمده ست چالاک و هشیار آمده ست
ورنه ببازارم چکار وی را طلب کار آمدم

۹   ای شمس تبریزی نظر در کلِّ عالم کی کنی؟
کاندر بیابان فنا جان و دل افگار آمدم

XXXIII ≈ [1390] - *I'VE RETURNED*

❖

1. *I*'VE returned, I've returned. I've come from the home of the [beloved.
Look at me, look at me. I am here out of compassion for you.
2. I've come with joy, I've come with joy, free from all things.
Thousands of years passed before I began to speak.
3. I shall go there, I shall go there. I was above the sky, I will go back.
Liberate me, liberate me. I am here for the covenant.
4. I was a divine bird, I became an earthly one.
I did not see the trap and was suddenly captured in it.
5. I am pure light, not a handful of unworthy dust.
I am the Kingly pearl, not mother of pearl.
6. Do not see me with the eye of the head. See me with the eye [of mystery.
Come and see me there, for there I am free of burden.
7. I am higher than the four mothers and the seven fathers[1].
In the mines of heaven I was a jewel who came here for a visit.
8. Nimble and alert my beloved came to the market.
What do I care about going to the market, except to search for [Him?
9. O Shams-i Tabrīz, when will you look upon the whole world?
In this wilderness of destruction, my heart and soul are afflicted.

۳۴ - [۱۳۹۳] - مرده بدم زنده شدم گریه بدم خنده شدم

❧

۱. مرده بدم زنده شدم گریه بدم خنده شدم
دولت عشق آمد و من دولت پاینده شدم

۲. دیدهٔ سیر است مرا جان دلیر است مرا
زَهرهٔ شیر است مرا زُهرهٔ تابنده شدم

۳. گفت: «که دیوانه نئی لایق این خانه نئی»
رفتم دیوانه شدم سلسله بندنده شدم

۴. گفت که: «سرمست نئی رو که ازین دست نئی»
رفتم و سر مست شدم وز طرب آکنده شدم

۵. گفت که: «تو کشته نئی در طرب آغشته نئی»
پیش رخ زنده کنش کشته و افکنده شدم

۶. گفت که: «تو زیرککی مست خیالی و شکی»
گول شدم هول شدم وز همه بر کنده شدم

۷. گفت که: «تو شمع شدی قبلهٔ این جمع شدی»
جمع نیم شمع نیم دود پراکنده شدم

۸. گفت که: «شیخی و سری پیشرو و راهبری»
شیخ نیم پیش نیم امر تو را بنده شدم

۹. گفت که: «با بال و پری من پرو بالت ندهم»
در هوس بال و پرش بی پر و پر کنده شدم

XXXIV = [1393] - *I WAS DEAD*

❦

1. *I* WAS dead, I became alive, I was tears, laughter, I became.
   The fortune of love arrived, eternal fortune I became.

2. My eyes are content, my soul is brave.
   Mine is the heart of a lion. The radiant Venus[1] I became.

3. He said: «You are not mad, you are not worthy of this house.»
   Insanity I chose, and was bound in chains.

4. He said: «You are not drunk – go away – you are not of our kind.»
   I went and got drunk, ecstatic I became.

5. He said: «You have not died, you are not drowned in ecstasy.»
   I died and fell at the feet of the one who revives.

6. He said: «You are cunning, you are drunk with fantasy and doubt.»
   I withdrew from all, a mute, a Sphinx I became.

7. He said: «You are a candle, the *qibla*[2] of this crowd you became.»
   I am not with the crowd, I am not a candle, scattered smoke
   [I became.

8. He said: «You are a *shaikh*, a head, a guide and a leader.»
   I am not a *shaikh*, not a leader. I am a slave to your command.

9. He said: «You have wings, I won't give you wings.»
   In the desire of his wings, wingless I became.

١٠   گفت مرا دولت نو: «راه مرو رنجه مشو
     زانکه من از لطف و کرم سوی تو آینده شدم»
١١   گفت مرا عشق کهن: «از بر ما نقل مکن»
     گفتم آری نکنم ساکن و باشنده شدم
١٢   چشمهٔ خورشید تویی سایه گه بید منم
     چون که زدی بر سر من پست و گدازنده شدم
١٣   تابش جان یافت دلم واشد و بشکافت دلم
     اطلس نو بافت دلم دشمن این ژنده شدم
١٤   صورت جان وقت سحر لاف همی زد ز بطر
     بنده و خربنده بدم شاه و خداونده شدم
١٥   شکر کند کاغذ تو از شکر بی حد نو
     کامد او در بر من با وی مانده شدم
١٦   شکر کند خاک دژم از فلک و چرخ به خم
     کز نظر و گردش او نور پذیرنده شدم
١٧   شکر کند چرخ فلک از مَلِک و مُلک و مَلَک
     کز کرم و بخشش او روشن و بخشنده شدم
١٨   شکر کند عارف حق کز همه بردیم سبق
     بر زبر هفت طبق اختر رخشنده شدم
١٩   از تو ام ای شهرهٔ قمر در من و در خود بنگر
     کز اثر خندهٔ تو گلشن خندنده شدم

✵

10. My newfound fortune told me: «Do not walk, do not toil,
    because out of mercy and compassion, I am coming towards
    [you.»
11. The ancient love said: «Do not remove yourself from me».
    I said: «I shall not.» I became quiescent and calm.
12. You are the source of the sun. I am the shade of the willow.
    Since your rays have fallen upon my head, humble and molten
    [I became.
13. My heart took on the luster of the soul. It expanded and split
    [open.
    My heart wove new silk, the enemy of this rag I became.
14. At the break of dawn, my soul boasted out of exultation:
    a slave and a donkey keeper I was, a king and a Lord I became.
15. The wrap around you is thankful for your infinite sweetness:
    «Since you came to my arms, like you I became.»
16. The sorrowful earth gives thanks to heaven and the curved dome,
    «Because of your revolving glance, a receptacle of light I became.»
17. All the creation, the King, kingdom and angels give thanks:
    «Because of Your magnanimity and grace, enlightened and giving
    [I became.»
18. The one who knows the truth gives thanks saying that: «I am
    [ahead of all.
    Above the seventh heaven a shining star I became.»
19. I am of you: O famous Moon, look in me and see yourself.
    Because of your laughter a laughing rose garden I became.

۲۵- [۱۴۳۹] - من این ایوان نه تو را نمی دانم نمی دانم

۱ من این ایوان نُه تو را نمی دانم نمی دانم
من این نقاش جادو را نمی دانم نمی دانم

۲ مراگوید: «مرو هر سو تو استادی بیا این سو»
که من آن سوی بی سو را نمی دانم نمی دانم

۳ همی گیرد گریبانم همی دارد پریشانم
من این خوش خوی بد خو را نمی دانم نمی دانم

۴ مرا جان طرب پیشه ست که بی مطرب نیارامد
من این جان طرب جو را نمی دانم نمی دانم

۵ یکی شیری همی بینم جهان پیشش گلهٔ آهو
که من این شیر و آهو را نمی دانم نمی دانم

۶ مرا سیلاب بربوده مرا جویای جو کرده
که این سیلاب و این جو را نمی دانم نمی دانم

۷ چو طفلی گم شدستم من میان کوی و بازاری
که این بازار و این کو را نمی دانم نمی دانم

۸ مرا گوید یکی مشفق: «بدت گویند بد گویان»
نکو گو را و بد گو را نمی دانم نمی دانم

XXXV ≈ [1439] - I DON'T KNOW THIS HOUSE

❧

1. *I* DON'T know this house of nine levels, I do not know it.
   I don't know this sorcerer-image maker, I do not know Him.
2. He tells me: «Do not go in every direction. You are a master
   [come this way.»
   But I don't know that directionless direction. I do not know it.
3. He grabs me by the collar, He bewilders me.
   I don't know this kind and cruel one. I do not know Him.
4. My soul is a lover of joy, which cannot rest without a minstrel.
   I don't know this joy loving soul. I do not know it.
5. I see a lion. To him the whole world is a herd of deer.
   I don't know this lion and these deer. I do not know them.
6. I was caught up in a current. It made me seek the river.
   But I don't know this current or this river. I do not know them.
7. I am like a lost child in the alleys and the market.
   But I don't know this market and these alleys. I do not know
   [them.
8. A kind friend tells me: I am being bad mouthed by the gossips.
   I don't know a kind friend from a gossip. I do not distinguish.

۹ زمین چون زن فلک چون شو خورد فرزند چون گربه
من این زن را و این شو را نمی دانم نمی دانم

۱۰ مرا آن صورت غیبی به ابرو نکته می گوید
که غمزهٔ چشم و ابرو را نمی دانم نمی دانم

۱۱ منم یعقوب و اویوسف که چشمم روشن ازبویش
اگرچه اصل این بو را نمی دانم نمی دانم

۱۲ جهان گررو ترش دارد چو مه درروی من خندد
که من جز میر مه رو را نمی دانم نمی دانم

۱۳ ز دست و بازوی قدرت به هر دم تیغ می پرد
که من آن دست و بازو را نمی دانم نمی دانم

۱۴ دکان نانبا دیدم که قرصش قرص ماه آمد
س این نان و ترازو را نمی دانم نمی دانم

۱۵ توگویی: «شش جهت منگربه سوی بی سویی برپر»
بیا این سو من آن سو را نمی دانم نمی دانم

۱۶ بروای شب زپیش من مپیچان زلف وگیسو را
که جز آن جعد و گیسو را نمی دانم نمی دانم

۱۷ بروای روزگل چهره که خورشیدت چه گلگون است
که من جز نور یا هو را نمی دانم نمی دانم

۱۸ دلم چون تیر می پَرَّد کمان تن همی غُرَّد
اگرآن دست و بازورا نمی دانم نمی دانم

۱۹ بیا ای شمس تبریزی مکن سنگین دلی با من
که با تو سنگ و لولو را نمی دانم نمی دانم

9. The earth is like a woman, the sky her husband, who eats its
   [offspring like a cat.
   I don't know this woman and her husband. I do not know them.

10. That invisible face emphasizes his point with his eyebrows.
    But I don't know about the allusions of the eyes and the eyebrows.
    [I do not know.

11. I am Jacob, he is Joseph. My eyes gain sight from his smell.
    However I don't know the origin of this smell. I do not know it.

12. The world, in all of its cruelty, smiles at me like the moon.
    Because I don't know anything, but that moon in its royal splendor.

13. Every moment arrows fly at me from the hand and the
    [arm of the mighty One.
    But I don't know that hand and that arm. I do not know them.

14. In the baker's shop I saw the loaf rising like the moon.
    I do not know this loaf or this scale. I do not know them.

15. You say: «Don't look towards the six directions. Fly toward the
    [place of no direction.»
    You come this way. I don't know that direction. I do not know it.

16. Be gone, O night. Do not twirl your locks in front of me.
    I don't know any lock of hair but that one. I do not know.

17. Be gone O rosy-cheeked day, how splendid is your sunlight.
    I don't know any light but the light of *yā hū*[1]. I do not know.

18. My heart flies like an arrow. The bow of my body roars,
    although I don't know that hand or that arm. I do not know them.

19. Come O Shams-i Tabrīz. Do not be stonehearted with me.
    With you, I don't distinguish a stone from a pearl. I do not know.

۲۶- [۱۴۴۷] - رفتم به طبیب جان گفتم که: «ببین د ستم

۱ فتم به طبیب جان گفتم که: «ببین دستم
هم بی دل و بیمارم هم عاشق و سر مستم

۲ صد گونه خلل دارم ای کاش یکی بودی
با این همه علّت ها در شنقصه پیوستم»

۳ گفتا که: «نه تو مَردی؟» گفتم که: «بلی اما
چون بوی توام آمد از کور برون جستم»

۴ آن صورت روحانی وان مشرق یزدانی
وآن یوسف کنعانی کز وی کف خود خستم

۵ خوش خوش سوی من آمد دستی به دلم بر زد
گفتا: «زچه دستی تو؟» گفتم که: «ازین دستم»

۶ چون عربده می کردم درداد می وخوردم
افروخت رخ زردم وز عربده وارستم

۷ پس جامه برون کردم مستانه جنون کردم
در حلقهٔ آن مستان درمیمنه بنشستم

۸ صد جام بنوشیدم صد گونه بجوشیدم
صد کاسه بریزیدم صدکوزه دراشکستم

۹ گوسالهٔ زرّین را آن قوم پرستیده
گوسالهٔ گرگینم گر عشق بنپرستم

DĪVĀN-I SHAMS-I TABRĪZ

XXXVI ≈ [1447] - *I WENT TO THE PHYSICIAN*

❧

1. *I* WENT to the physician of the soul and said: «Look at my state;
   I am heart broken and sick, at the same time drunk and in love.

2. I have hundreds of flaws. I wish it were only one.
   It is with all these faults that I became a seeker of the truth.»

3. He said: «Didn't you die?» I said: «Yes,
   but when I smelled your scent I jumped out of the grave.»

4. That holy face, that Godly rising sun,
   that Joseph of Canaan[1] who caused me to wound my hand,

5. came to me with charm and grace, touched my heart,
   and said: «Where do you belong?» I said: «I belong here.»

6. Since I was brawling, he gave me a cup of wine.
   My sallow face burst aflame and I was free of quarrel.

7. Then I shed my clothes, I became like an insane drunkard
   and I sat in the circle of the drunkards, in happiness.

8. I drank a hundred cups, I burned in a hundred ways.
   I spilled a hundred goblets, I broke a hundred jugs.

9. That tribe worshiped the golden calf.
   I'd be a mangy calf if I didn't worship love.

۱ بازم شه روحانی می خواند پنهانی
بر میکشدم بالا شاهانه ازین پستم

۲ پا بست توام جانا سرمست توام جانا
پست توام ار پستم هست توام ارهستم

۳ در چرخ در آوردی چون مست خودم کردی
چون تو سرِ خُم بستی من نیز دهان بستم

10 The King of the spirit is secretly calling me back.
   He is pulling me up like a King from this pit.

11 O my soul, I am chained to you. I am drunk of you.
   If I am ruined, it is because of you. If I am, it's because of you.

12 You took me to heaven when you got me drunk.
   When you covered the jar of wine I closed my mouth.

۲۷ - [۱۵۰۲] - زندان خلق را آزاد کردم

۱ ز زندان خلق را آزاد کردم
وان عاشقان را شاد کردم

۲ دهان اژدها را بردریدم
طریق عشق را آباد کردم

۳ ز آبی من جهانی برتنیدم
پس آنکه آب را پرباد کردم

۴ ببستم نقش ها بر آب کان را
نه بر عاج و نه بر شمشاد کردم

۵ زهی باغی که من ترتیب کردم
زهی شهری که من بنیاد کردم

۶ جهان داند که تا من شاه اویم
بدادم داد مُلک و داد کردم

۷ جهان داند که بیرون از جهانم
تصور بهر استشهاد کردم

۸ چه استادان که من شه مات کردم
چه شاگردان که من استاد کردم

۹ بسا شیران که غرَّیدند بر ما
چو روبه عاجز و منقاد کردم

XXXVII ≈ [1502] - *I LIBERATED THE PEOPLE*

1. *I* LIBERATED the people from prison.
   I lifted the spirits of the lovers.
2. I ripped out the mouth of the dragon.
   I cleared the path of love.
3. I wove a world from water.
   Then I blew breath into the water.
4. I carved such images in the water,
   that I never carved in ivory or boxwood.
5. I designed a marvelous garden.
   I founded a marvelous city.
6. The world knows that when I am its king,
   I'll rule fairly and dispense justice throughout the land.
7. The world knows that I am outside the world.
   Consider this as my testimonial.
8. I checkmated many masters.
   I made masters out of many students.
9. So many lions who roared at me,
   I bound and subdued as though they were foxes.

۱۰ خمش کن آن که اوازصُلب عشق است
بسستش این که من ارشاد کردم

۱۱ ولیک آن را که طوفان بلا بُرد
فرو شد گر چه من فریاد کردم

۱۲ مگر از قعر طوفانش بر آرم
چنان که نیست را ایجاد کردم

۱۳ بر آمد شمس تبریزی بزد تیغ
زبان از تیغ او پولاد کردم

※

10 Be silent, for the one who sprang from the seed of love,
the guidance I gave is enough.

11 But the one who was taken away by the cyclone of evil,
was swallowed up no matter how much I screamed.

12 Yet I may release him from the heart of the cyclone,
the way I brought nothingness into existence.

13 Shams-i Tabrīz came and struck with his sword.
My tongue became steel from the power of his blade.

۲۸ - [۱۵۱۶] - چه نزدیک است جان تو به جانم

۱ چه نزدیک است جان تو به جانم
که هر چیزی که اندیشی بدانم

۲ ضمیر همدگر دانند یاران،
نباشم یار صادق گر ندانم

۳ چو آب صاف باشد یار با یار
که بنماید در او عکس بنانم

۴ اگر چه عامه هم آیینه هایند
که بنماید در او سود و زیانم

۵ ولیکن آن به هر دم تیره گردد
که او را نیست صیقل های جانم

۶ ولی آیینهٔ عارف نگردد
اگر خاک جهان بروی فشانم

۷ ازین آیینه روی خود مگردان
که می گوید که جانت را امانم

۸ من و گفت من آیینه ست جان را
بیابد حال خویش اندر بیانم

۹ خمش کن تا به ابروو به غمزه
هزاران ماجرا بر وی بخوانم

XXXVIII ≈ [1516] - *Your Soul is so Close*

1. *Y*OUR soul is so close to mine,
   that whatever you think, I know.

2. Friends know each other's hearts.
   I wouldn't be a true friend if I didn't know yours.

3. A friend to a friend is like still water,
   reflecting the truth back to one another.

4. Even though all men are mirrors,
   reflecting gains and losses,

5. at any moment they may be tarnished,
   as they lack the luster from my soul.

6. If you darken the mirror, with the dust of the world,
   it will never reflect the light of knowledge[1].

7. Do not turn your face from this mirror,
   for it says: «I am the refuge of your soul.»

8. I and my words are mirrors for the soul,
   Who's state is reflected in my expression.

9. Be silent, for by allusion and innuendo,
   I will tell a thousand stories.

۳۹- [۱۵۱۷] - مرا گویی: «کرایی؟» من چه دانم

❋

۱   مرا گویی: «کرایی؟» من چه دانم
      «چنین مجنون چرایی؟» من چه دانم

۲   مرا گویی: «بدین زاری که هستی
      به عشقم چون برآیی؟» من چه دانم

۳   منم در موج دریاهای عشقت
      مرا گویی: «کجایی؟» من چه دانم

۴   مرا گویی: «به قربانگاه جان‌ها
      نمی‌ترسی که آیی؟» من چه دانم

۵   مرا گویی: «اگر کشتهٔ خدایی
      چه داری از خدایی؟» من چه دانم

۶   مرا گویی: «چه می‌جویی دگر تو
      ورای روشنایی؟» من چه دانم

۷   مرا گویی: «ترا با این قفس چیست
      اگر مرغ هوایی؟» من چه دانم

۸   مرا راه صوابی بود گم شد
      از آن ترک خطایی من چه دانم

۹   بلا را از خوشی نشناسم ایرا
      به غایت خوش بلایی من چه دانم

۱۰   شبی بربود ناگه شمس تبریز
      ز من یک تا دو تایی من چه دانم

❋

XXXIX ≈ [1517] - YOU ASK ME

❧

1. *Y*OU ask me: «Who do you belong to?» What do I know?
   You ask me: «Why are you such a madman?» What do I know?

2. You ask me: «How, so weak and infirmed,
   can you ascend to love me?» What do I know?

3. I am tossed by the waves in the ocean of your love.
   You ask me: «Where are you?» What do I know?

4. You ask me: «Aren't you afraid to come,
   to the place of the soul's sacrifice?» What do I know?

5. You ask me: «If you are a sacrifice for God,
   what signs of Godliness do you have?» What do I know?

6. You ask me: «What else do you seek,
   beyond illumination?» What do I know?

7. You ask me: «Why are you in this cage,
   if you are a bird of the sky?» What do I know?

8. I was walking on a good path but I lost my way
   on account of that Turk of Khatā[1]. What do I know?

9. Now I do not distinguish adversity from pleasure.
   You are the ultimate in pleasurable adversity. What do I know?

10. Suddenly, one night, Shams-i Tabrīz stole away
    my unique duality. What do I know?

۴۰ - [۱۵۱۹] - بیا کامروز بیرون از جهانم

۱. بیا کامروز بیرون از جهانم
بیا کامروز من از خود نهانم

۲. گرفتم دشنه ای وز خود بریدم
نه آنِ خود نه آنِ دیگرانم

۳. غلط کردم نبریدم من از خود
که این تدبیر بی من کرد جانم

۴. ندانم کآتش دل بر چه سان است
که دیگر شکل می سوزد زبانم

۵. به صد صورت بدیدم خویشتن را
به هر صورت همی گفتم من آنم

۶. همی گفتم مرا صد صورت آمد
و یا صورت نیم من بی نشانم

۷. که صورت های دل چون میهمانند
که می آیند و من چون خانه بانم

DĪVĀN-I SHAMS-I TABRĪZ

XL ≈ 1519 - COME, FOR TODAY

1. COME, for today I am outside the world.
   Come, for today I am hidden from myself.

2. I took a dagger and cut myself from me.
   I belong neither to myself nor to others.

3. No, I am wrong; I didn't cut myself from me,
   My soul did this deed without me.

4. I don't know how my heart's flame
   ignites my tongue, which burns so differently.

5. I saw myself in a thousand different forms.
   In each form, I said: «That is who I am.»

6. I asked: «Do I have a thousand forms,
   or am I formless and without trace?»

7. The forms of the heart are guests
   come visiting, and I am their host.

۴۱ - [۱۵۳۵] - بیا تا قدر همدیگر بدانیم

۱. بیا تا قدر همدیگر بدانیم
که تا ناگه ز یکدیگر نمانیم

۲. چو مؤمن آینهٔ مؤمن یقین شد
چرا با آینهٔ ما رو گرانیم؟

۳. کریمان جان فدای دوست کردند
سگی بگذار ما هم مردمانیم

۴. فسون قُل اَعُوذ و قُل هُوَ اللّه
چرا در عشق همدیگر نخوانیم

۵. غرض‌ها تیره دارد دوستی را
غرض‌ها را چرا از دل نرانیم؟

۶. گهی خوش دل شوی از من که میرم
چرا مرده پرست و خصم جانیم؟

۷. چو بعد از مرگ خواهی آشتی کرد
همه عمر از غمت در امتحانیم

۸. کنون پندار مُردَم آشتی کن
که در تسلیم ما چون مردگانیم

۹. چو بر گورم بخواهی بوسه دادن
رُخَم را بوسه ده کاکنون همانیم

۱۰. خمش کن مرده وار ای دل ازیرا
به هستی مُتَّهَم ما زین زبانیم

DĪVĀN-I SHAMS-I TABRĪZ

XLI = [1535] - COME, LET'S APPRECIATE

❧

1. COME, let's appreciate each other,
   before we suddenly miss each other.
2. Since it is certain that: «The believer is the mirror for the
   believer[1],» why must we turn our face from the mirror?
3. The generous beings sacrificed their life for the friend.
   Quit being a dog, we are also human beings.
4. Why don't we sing out of love, for each other,
   the magic of: «Say, I seek refuge…» and «Say, He is God…»[2]
5. Rancor darkens friendship.
   Why not cast rancor from our hearts?
6. You will be happy with me when I die.
   Why are we worshipers of the dead and enemies of the living?
7. Since you would want to make peace after I die,
   while alive I am forever on trial for you.
8. Imagine now that I am dead, and so make peace.
   I am like a corpse in surrender.
9. Since you would want to kiss my grave,
   instead kiss my face. I am dead now.
10. O heart, like a dead man, be silent,
    because of this tongue I am accused of existence[3].

۴۲ - [۱۵۲۶] - میان ما در آ ما عاشقانیم

۱   میان ما در آ ما عاشقانیم
     که تا در باغ عشقت در کشانیم

۲   مقیم خانهٔ ما شو چو سایه
     که ما خورشید را همسایگانیم

۳   چو جان اندر جهان گر ناپدیدیم
     چو عشق عاشقان گر بی نشانیم

۴   ولیک آثار ما پیوستهٔ تست
     که ما چون جان نهانیم و عیانیم

۵   هر آن چیزی که تو گویی که آنید
     به بالاتر نگر بالای آنیم

۶   تو آبی لیک گردابی و محبوس
     در آ در ما که ما سیل روانیم

۷   چو ما در فقر مطلق پاک بازیم
     به جز تصنیف نادانی ندانیم

XLII ≈ [1536] ~ *COME AMONGST US*

1. COME amongst us, we are the lovers,
   who will take you to the garden of love.
2. In our house reside like a shadow.
   For we are neighbors with the sun.
3. Although we are, like spirits, invisible in the world,
   as ineffable as the love of true lovers,
4. still our essence flows from you,
   for, like the spirit, we are seen and yet not seen.
5. Whatever you say we are,
   we are above it, look higher.
6. You are water, but a vortex too, therefore a prisoner.
   Come amongst us. We are a river, we flow.
7. Since we are pure souls, lost in the poverty of the absolute,
   all we know is the song of ignorance.

۴۳ - [۱۵۷۷] - امروز نیم ملول شادم

۱   امروز نیم ملول شادم
غم را همه طاق برنهادم

۲   بر سبلت هر کجا ملولست
گر میر منست و اوستادم

۳   امروز میان به عیش بستم
روبند ز روی مه کشادم

۴   امروز ظریفم و لطیفم
گویی که مگر ز لطف زادم

۵   یاری که نداد بوسه از نار
او بوسه بجست و من ندادم

۶   من دوش عجب چه خواب دیدم
کامروز عظیم با مرادم

۷   گفتی تو که: «رو که پادشاهی»
آری که خوش و خجسته بادم

۸   بی ساقی و بی شراب مستم
بی بخت و کلاه کیقبادم

۹   در من ز کجا رسد گمان ها
سبحان الله کجا فتادم!

XLIII ≈ [1577] - *Today I'm not Gloomy*

1. *T*ODAY I'm not gloomy, I'm happy.
   I've put all sorrows in the attic.

2. Away with whoever is gloomy
   whether he is my prince or my master.

3. Today my mind is set on happiness,
   I took the veil off the face of the moon.

4. Today I am witty and wise,
   you'd say I was born of knowledge.

5. The lover who did not give me a kiss out of coyness,
   sought to kiss me but I did not let her.

6. Last night I had a marvelous dream
   I saw that I will achieve my wish.

7. You told me: «Go, you are a King.»
   Yes, I am blessed and fortunate.

8. I am drunk without *sāqi*[1] and wine.
   I am Kay Qubād[2] without a crown and a throne.

9. From where do these ideas come to me?
   Praise God, where am I?

۴۴ - [۱۵۸۵] - ای جهان آب و گل تا من ترا بشناختم

۱. ای جهان آب و گل تا من ترا بشناختم
صد هزاران محنت و رنج و بلا بشناختم

۲. تو چراگاه خرانی نی مقام عیسیی
این چراگاه خران را من چرا بشناختم؟

۳. آب شیرینم ندادی تا که خوان گسترده ای
دست و پایم بسته ای تا دست و پا بشناختم

۴. دست و پا را چون نبندی گاهواره ت خواند حق
دست و پا را بر گشایم پاگشا بشناختم

۵. چون درخت از زیر خاکی دست ها بالا کنم
در هوای آن کسی کز وی هوا بشناختم

۶. ای شکوفه تو به طفلی چون شدی پیر تمام؟
گفت: «رستم از صبا تا من صَبا بشناختم»

۷. شاخ بالا زان رود زیرا ز بالا آمده ست
سوی اصل خویش یازم کاصل را بشناختم

۸. زیر و بالا چند گویم لامکان اصل من است
من نه از جایم کجا را از کجا بشناختم؟

۹. نی خمش کن در عدم رو در عدم نا چیز شو
چیز ها را بین که از ناچیز ها بشناختم

DĪVĀN-I SHAMS-I TABRĪZ

XLIV ≈ [1585] - O WORLD OF WATER AND MUD

⚜

1. *O* WORLD of water and mud, since I've known you,
   I've known a hundred thousand torments, trials and tribulations.

2. You are the grazing field for the donkeys, you are not the abode [of Jesus.
   Why did I get to know this grazing field for the donkeys?

3. You never gave me sweet water since you spread your banquet.
   You have tied my hands and feet since I became aware of hands [and feet.

4. How could you not tie up my hands and feet, since God called [you the cradle[1].
   But I will untie my hands and feet. I found the freedom giver

5. Like a tree I will raise my hands up from under the soil,
   seeking the one who made the sky.

6. O blossom, how did you become so wise at infancy?
   She said: «I was free of childhood from the moment the lover's [breeze[2] touched me.»

7. The branch goes up because it came from above.
   I am drawn to my source because I know the source.

8. How long do I say down and up? My source is the place of [no place.
   I am not from any place, how do I know 'where,' where is?

9. No, be silent, go to nothingness and in nothingness become [nothing.
   And behold things, the way I came to know them in nothingness.

✹

۴۵ - [۱۵۸۶] - خویش را چون خار دیدم سوی گل بگریختم

۱ خویش را چون خار دیدم سوی گل بگریختم
خویش را چون سرکه دیدم در شکر آمیختم

۲ کاسهٔ پر زهر بودم سوی تریاق آمدم
ساغری دُردی بدم در آب حیوان ریختم

۳ دیدهٔ پر درد بودم دست در عیسی زدم
خام دیدم خویش را در پخته ای آویختم

۴ خاک کوی عشق را من سرمهٔ جان یافتم
شعر گشتم در لطافت سُرمه را می بیختم

۵ عشق گوید: «راست می گویی ولی از خود مبین
من چو بادم تو چو آتش من تو را انگیختم»

XLV = [1586] - *I Saw Myself as a Thorn*

1. *I* saw myself as a thorn, I ran to the rose.
   I saw myself as vinegar, I mixed with sugar.
2. I was a bowl full of poison, I went for the antidote[1].
   I was a cup full of dregs, I mixed in with the water of life.
3. I was a blinded eye, I reached for the hand of Jesus.
   I saw myself as crude, I clung to someone mature.
4. I found the dust of the alley of love to be collyrium of the soul[2].
   I became a hair, I sifted collyrium with grace.
5. Love says: «You speak the truth, but don't think it comes from you.
   I am like wind, you are like fire. I stirred you up.»

۴۶ - [۱۷۰۳] - من آن شب سیاهم کز ماه خشم کردم

۱   من آن شب سیاهم کز ماه خشم کردم
     من آن گدای عورم کزشاه خشم کردم

۲   از لطفم آن یگانه می خواند سوی خانه
     کردم یکی بهانه وز راه خشم کردم

۳   گر سر کشد نگارم ور غم برد قرارم
     هم آه بر نیارم از آه خشم کردم

۴   گاهم فریفت با زر گاهم به جاه و لشکر
     از زر چو زر بجستم وز جاه خشم کردم

۵   ز آهن ربای اعظم من آهنم گریزان
     وز کهربای عالم من کاه خشم کردم

۶   ما ذرّه ایم سرکش از چار و پنج و از شش
     خود پنج و شش چه باشد ز اللّه خشم کردم

۷   این را تو بر نتابی زیرا برون آبی
     گر شبه آفتابی ز اشباه خشم کردم

DĪVĀN-I SHAMS-I TABRĪZ

XLVI ≈ [1703] - *I AM THE BLACK NIGHT*

⚜

1. *I* AM the black night who raged against the moon;
   I am the naked beggar who raged against the king.
2. He the Singular in His Munificence summoned me home;
   Offering excuses, I raged against the journey.
3. If my beloved rebels, if sorrow robs me of peace,
   not a sigh escapes me, for I rage against sighs.
4. Sometimes he tempted me with gold, sometimes with position [and rank,
   I fled from gold like the rising sun[1], I raged against the rank.
5. Iron though I am, I shun the great magnet;
   A mere straw, I evade the amber[2] of the universe.
6. I am a particle, rebel to the four, five and six[3];
   Of what consequence is four, five and six, when I raged against [God?
7. This is unbearable to you, for you are not swimming in this [ocean;
   Even if you resemble the sun, I rage against your resemblance.

۴۷ - [۱۸۱۰] - من دزد دیدم کو برد مال و متاع مردمان

❊

۱   من دزد دیدم کو برد مال و متاع مردمان
    این دزد ما خود دزدرا چون می بدزدد از میان؟

۲   خواهند از سلطان امان چون دزد افزونی کند
    دزدی چو سلطان می کند پس از کجا خواهند امان؟

۳   عشق است آن سلطان که او از جمله دزدان دل برد
    تا پیش آن سرکش برد حق سرکشان را مو کشان

۴   عشق است آن دزدی که اواز شحنگان دل می برد
    در خدمت آن دزد بین تو شحنگان بی کران

۵   آواز دادم دوش من کای خفتگان دزد آمده ست
    دزدیداواز چابکی در حین زبانم از دهان

۶   گفتم ببندم دست او خود بست او دستان من
    گفتم به زندانش کنم او می نگنجد در جهان

۷   از لذّت دزدی او هر پاسبان دزدی شده
    از حیله و دستان او هر زیرکی گشته نهان

۸   خلقی ببینی نیمشب جمع آمده کان دزد کو
    اونیز می پرسد که: «کوآن دزد؟» او خوددر میان

XLVII = [1810] – *I Saw a Thief*

❧

1. *I* saw a thief who robbed people of their property and wealth.
   How can this thief steal from the belly of thieves?
2. They complain to the Sultan when the thieves go to excess,
   but who do you complain to when the Sultan is the thief?
3. The Truth drags the rebellious ones by the hair to meet the
   [All-powerful One,
   for love is that Sultān which steals the hearts of all thieves.
4. Love is the thief who steals the heart of all the sentries.
   Look at the countless sentries who serve that thief.
5. Last night I cried: «O, sleepy ones, the thief is here».
   Then and there, he swiftly stole my tongue from my mouth.
6. I said: I'll tie his hands, but instead he tied mine.
   I said I shall imprison him; not even the entire world could
   [contain him.
7. From delighting so much in his thievery all the guards became
   [thieves.
   Every ingenious man hid from his deceit and duplicity.
8. In the middle of the night, you see the crowd asking: «Where
   [is the thief?»
   Standing amongst them, he also asks: «Where is the thief?»

٩ ای مایهٔ هر گفت و گو ای دشمن وای دوست رو
ای هم حیات جاودان ای هم بلای ناگهان

١٠ ای رفته اندر خون دل ای ترا کرده به حلّ
بر من بزن زخم و مهل حقًّا نمی خواهم امان

١١ سخته کمانی خوش بکش بر من بزن آن تیر خوش
ای من فدای تیر تو ای من غلام آن کمان

١٢ زخم تو در رگ های من جانست و جان افزای من
شمشیر تو بر نای من حیفست ای شاه جهان

١٣ شه شمس تبریزی مگر باز چون آیداز سفر
یک چند بود اندر بشر شد همچو عنقا بی نشان

9. O, you who are the subject of all talk. O, enemy with the face
[of a friend,
   O, eternal life and, then again, sudden disaster.
10. O, creator of the bleeding heart, O, soother of the broken
[heart,
    do not stop inflicting wounds upon me. God knows I ask for
[no quarter.
11. O, great archer, draw your bow and strike me with that sweet
[arrow.
    Let me be the sacrifice to your arrow, I am the slave of your bow.
12. The wounds that you inflict upon me give blood to my
[veins and life to my soul,
    my throat is not worthy of your sword, O, king of the world.
13. Perhaps Shams-i Tabrīz, like a falcon, will come back.
    For a time, he was manifest in a man, then he became traceless
[like the *Anqā*[1].

۴۸ - [۲۶۷۰] - خوشی آخر بگو ای یار چونی

۱ خوشی آخر بگو ای یار چونی
از این ایّام نا هموار چونی؟

۲ به روز و شب مرا اندیشهٔ توست
کزین روز و شب خون خوار چونی

۳ ازین آتش که در عالم فتاده ست
ز دود لشکر تاتار چونی؟

۴ درین دریا و تاریکی و صد موج
تو اندر کشتی پر بار چونی؟

۵ صنم بیمار و تو مارا طبیبی
بپرس آخر که ای بیمار چونی

۶ منت پرسم اگر تو می نپرسی
که ای شیرین شیرین کار چونی

۷ وجودی بین که بی چون و چگونه ست
دلا دیگر مگو بسیار چونی

۸ بگو در گوش شمس الدّین تبریز
که ای خورشید خوب اسرار چونی

XLVIII = [2670] - *Are You well, my Love?*

❧

1. *A*re you well, my love? Tell me how you are.
   With these times of adversity, how are you?
2. I think about you day and night,
   with these bloodthirsty days and nights, I wonder, how are you.
3. With this fire that engulfs the world,
   with the smoke wrought by the armies of the Tartars, how are you?
4. In this sea, surrounded by darkness and a thousand waves,
   In a heavily laden ship, how are you?
5. I am afflicted and you are my physician.
   Ask me, the afflicted one: «How are you?»
6. I ask you even if you don't ask me,
   O sweet one with sweet deeds, how are you?
7. Behold the wonderful and unequalled one.
   O heart, ask no more, how are you?
8. Whisper in the ear of Shams-i Tabrīz,
   O sun with beautiful secrets, how are you?

Zoomorphic Basmalah,
Turkey, nineteenth century.

Ghazal I.

[1] *Sāqi,* cupbearer. Usually a beautiful young man, who would make the rounds of the customers in the tavern with the cup of wine and control the drinkers. *Sāqi* is used profusely in Persian mystical poetry and often represents the beloved, the spiritual teacher or even the face of God.

[2] When Moses came to the appointed place and his Lord spoke to him, he asked God: «Show me yourself, so I can look upon you.» God replied: «You can never see me. Look upon the mountain; if the mountain remains in its place, you can see me.» When God revealed Himself to the mountain it shattered and Moses fell unconscious. When he recovered his senses he said: «Praise to You. I repent and turn to You, and I am the first to believe.» (Qur'ān, VII: 143).

Ghazal II.

[1] The Persian reads: «If you are Qārūn…», Qārūn was: «Of the people of Moses; but acted insolently towards them.» (Qur'ān, XXVIII: 76). Qārūn, like Croesus, possessed boundless treasures. He attributed his wealth to his own knowledge and not the will of God. So his pride caused him to be destroyed: «Then We caused the earth to swallow him and his house […]» (Qur'ān, XXVIII: 81).

[2] *Shams-i Tabrīzi,* pronounced as *Shams-e Tabrīzi* (The Tabrizian sun) and referred to also as *Shams-i Tabrīz* (The sun of Tabrīz) or *Shamseddin,* is the beloved spiritual teacher and friend of Rūmī who changed his life. See «Introduction».

Ghazal III.

[1] *Daf,* a percussion musical instrument; a handheld drum made of a wooden ring and sheepskin, similar to the Irish or the American Indian drum.

[2] *Nay,* a flute made out of a simple piece of reed with holes, about two feet long, with a soft and melodic sound.

Ghazal V.

[1] *Shesh jihat*, the six directions: East; West; North; South; Up; Down.

[2] *Mansūr*. This *bayt* refers to Husayn ibn Mansūr al-Hallāj (857-922 A.D.), the famous sūfī martyr who came to symbolize the ecstasy, as well as the suffering, of the lover's personal union with God. His fault, according to sūfī tradition, was that he revealed his secret (*ana'l-haq* [I am the Truth]) to unworthy people of the world. *Haq* has many meanings, two of which are God and Truth. This statement is the ultimate expression of complete union with God, which has sometimes been uttered differently by others. For this heresy against orthodox interests and for political reasons, Husayn was sentenced to death during the reign of the caliph al-Muqtadir. After a long imprisonment, he was tied to the stake and dismembered. Tradition tells us he danced all the way to his martyrdom.

[3] *Ashiqān-I durd kish*, dreg drinking lovers. The poor drink the worst type of wine, the dregs; lovers are poor, lovers drink dregs. This expression could also read *dard kish*, meaning sufferer.

[4] *Fanā'*, annihilation. The ultimate goal of a mystic is to become annihilated in God, therefore returning to the source. The metaphor for such a transformation, employed frequently in Persian poetry, is a moth being burned by a candle flame, thus becoming one with it.

[5] *Hasti*, being, existence (antonym: *nīsti*, non existence) would be the normal condition of human beings. It is the state of being overwhelmed by the imperious self (or ego) and far from the consciousness of God.

Ghazal VI.

[1] In the early days of Islām, Uways al-Qarani was one of the followers, away from the Prophet, in Yemen. He was very poor and made a living by taking care of other peoples' camels. With his wages he fed himself and his old mother, and he gave the rest to people poorer than himself. Farīd ad-dīn 'Attār (XI century), in his *Tadhqīrat-al Awliyā*, considers him the closest follower of the Prophet; he loved him more than all the others without physically having seen him. Uways knew every detail that happened to him, in Mecca or Medina. The finest agate, a semiprecious stone, worn often and honored by Muslims, comes from Yemen. Quite frequently in Persian poetry we see references to Yemen, Uways and agate. In this case, Uways goes unmentioned, but we know that by «priceless agate» the poet means none but Uways.

Ghazal VII.

[1] *Bād-i Sabā*, the wind that blows at dawn from the East. It is believed to be auspicious: the carrier of news from the beloved; reviver of plants in spring; and, especially, of blossoming flowers. «Lovers breeze» seems to be an appropriate translation.

[2] *Hajj*. One of the duties of every Muslim is to travel to Mecca for pilgrimage, at least once in his or her lifetime, if finances allow it. The proper time for the pilgrimage is in the month of *dhul-hajja* of the Muslim calendar.

DĪVĀN-I SHAMS-I TABRĪZ ❖ NOTES

³ *Mount Safa*, the mount of purity, is a large rock in Mecca. It is part of the *hajj* ritual to climb it to complete the pilgrimage.

⁴ *Shi'rā*, Sirius, the most brilliant star observed, a member of the constellation Canis Major. Also, dog-star.

Ghazal VIII.

¹ The original *bayt* reads: *Āmad bahār-i jānhā...* meaning: «The spring of souls is here...». Since in other editions of the *Dīvān* the third word is *janā*, meaning «My soul» instead of *jānhā*, I took the liberty of choosing the latter meaning.

² Joseph [Yūsuf], son of Jacob, is mentioned frequently in Persian poetry. He often represents the beloved, the symbol of ultimate Divine beauty and magnificence. For many centuries sugar was a precious commodity around the world. The best sugar came from Egypt. People who traveled from Egypt to other regions brought sugar cones for loved ones or important people. Often in Persian poetry we see Joseph, Egypt and sugar used as related words.

³ Literally translates: «You saw the mallet of the curl, you arrived as the polo ball. You gave up your head and feet, without feet and head begin to dance». Polo was a popular sport in Persian courts. The metaphor of the curved mallet of polo is used often in Persian poetry, representing the curl of the beloved, which tosses the head of the lover wherever it pleases.

⁴ *Khūni*, both «bloody» and «killer». So the first *misra'* (hemistich) of the *bayt* could mean: «The killer, with a sword in his hand...».

⁵ *Hasti*, existence. See *Ghazal* V⁵.

⁶ *Fanā*, annihilation. See *Ghazal* V⁴.

⁷ Literally the second *misra'* [hemistich] reads: «Separation has taken away my color and effect...».

⁸ Here *fanā* is used in the negative sense of death and destruction.

Ghazal XI.

¹ *Faliq ul-asbāh*, He is the one who cleaveth the day-break... (Qur'ān, VI: 96).

² *Rabb ul-falaq*, Lord of the Dawn... (Qur'ān, CXIII: 1).

³ *Kahrubā*, amber, literally the «attractor of straw». In general, *kahrubā* represents a magnet. In contemporary Arabic *kahrubā* means electricity.

⁴ *Hira*, a mountain near Mecca, where the prophet Muhammad went in seclusion to prepare for his prophetic mission.

⁵ *Sāqi*. See *Ghazal* I¹.

⁶ Literally the second *misra'* reads «in the language of eternity *(baqā)*». Other editions read *laqā*. I chose the latter.

Ghazal XIII.

¹ *Nāma'i a'māl*. A book of the actions of mankind, supposed to be kept by guardian or observing angels, to be produced at the Day of Judgment (Cfr. Qur'ān, XVIII: 49 *et passim*).

Ghazal XIV.

[1] *Nargis,* narcissus, represents the beautiful eye of the beloved and sometimes it replaces the word «eye».

[2] The hair of the beloved is often compared to a lasso. Here we have the same allusion.

[3] The original Persian reads: «I disappeared from that moon's heap of wheat like a measuring cup. Today that moon found me in the depth of the storehouse».

Ghazal XV.

[1] *Mi'rāj,* A flight of steps, ladder, ascent. The journey of the prophet Muḥammad to heaven to meet with God.

[2] Literally the second *misra'* is: «[...] since I found out that my fortune has been dragging me».

Ghazal XVI.

[1] Literally the second *misra'* reads: «Every particle of the soil is drunk from the Tyrant Creator». One of the attributes of God is *Jabbār* which means tyrant, proud, conqueror, avenger and bonesetter.

Ghazal XVII.

[1] *Falcon drum,* a small drum used to call back the tamed falcon which usually perches on the king's forearm. The falcon going back to the king's forearm is a metaphor often used to illustrate 'the coming back of the soul to his original source'.

[2] *Lion of God,* one of the titles of 'Alī ibn ābu-Tālib, the son-in-law of the Prophet, first imām of the Shī'ites and the fourth caliph of Islam. This title refers to his bravery and righteousness.

[3] *Rostam,* a mythical hero whose deeds are told in the great Persian epic *Shāh-nāmeh* [The book of the Kings] by Ferdowsi.

[4] *Hoopoe (hudhud),* a bird. Mentioned in the Qur'ān, the hoopoe is a friend of king Solomon and brings him news from all over the world. It is the hoopoe which brings news about the queen of Sheba and her realm to Solomon.

Ghazal XVIII.

[1] *Mount Qāf,* an imaginary mountain which surrounds the world and has mystical properties.

Ghazal XIX.

[1] *Abū Lahab,* Father of the Flame, the nickname of an uncle of the Prophet. He was one of the most powerful enemies of the Prophet and Islam. The *sūra* CXI of the Qur'ān is about Abū Lahab and his wife.

Ghazal XXI.

[1] *Hajj.* See *Ghazal* VII[2].

DĪVĀN-I SHAMS-I TABRĪZ ♦ NOTES

² *Ka'ba,* any square building; the sanctuary of Mecca. All Muslims face the *ka'ba* for prayer..

Ghazal XXIV.

¹ *Daf.* See *Ghazal* III¹.

² *Kharābāt* (sing. *khrābeh*), ruins. Used frequently in Persian mystical poetry, notably in the poetry of Hāfiz. It is usually translated as 'tavern' in English. It is obviously part of common metaphors, like wine, *sāqi,* drunkard and so on, disputed over and over by mystics and skeptics. The former, argue that all the words are symbolic; the latter, maintain that their meaning is literal. Arguments aside, for a pious person a tavern is the worst place to be, the opposite of a mosque or a sûfi monastery. But for a mystical poet, a tavern can only be a place where one is closest to God, free of the religious shell and the hypocrisy of the clergy.

Ghazal XXV.

¹ *Daf.* See *Ghazal* III¹. Literally: «O, minstrel of the soul, since the *daf* is in your hand, play this tune that [sings] the beloved is drunk».

Ghazal XXVI.

¹ Literally: «The one with his soul/life in a bottle, who ran away from needles, is ready to sell/give his life to the blade of love».

² *Ka'ba.* See *Ghazal* XXI².

Ghazal XXVIII.

¹ *Zulfaqār,* the famous sword of 'Alī. The followers of 'Alī believe that the souls of the unbelievers, who died by his sword in the holy wars, were saved and went to paradise. This *bayt* refers to the same idea.

² In Persian, the second word of the second *misra'* can be read in two ways with opposite meanings: *kon* and *kan*. In the first case, the phrase means: «wear your clothes...»; in the second, «go naked...».

³ *Rowzan,* window, hole, opening. The old bathhouses had domed ceilings in which there was a round hole for light and ventilation.

⁴ *Lā-makān,* is the place of the deity, where there is no space and time, a state beyond our conception.

Ghazal XXIX.

¹ *Majnūn,* insane, is the title of Qays, the ultimate lover who became mad for the love of Laylā. The story of Laylā and Majnūn is mentioned over and over in Persian literature and is considered the ultimate love story that transcends earthly love and becomes symbolic of Divine love.

² In Persian literature Joseph [Yūsuf] is the symbol of divine beauty. The entire *sūra* XII of the Qur'ān (*sūra* of Joseph) has been dedicated to him. The mystical poets always refer to Joseph as if he were the face of God (*wajh-ullah*). After being saved from the well Joseph

was living at the house of the Egyptian dignitary whose wife fell in love with him. But he did not reciprocate so she accused him of the sin he had not committed. In verses 30 and 31 of the *sūra* of Joseph we read: «Around the city ladies said: "The wife of Azīz wants to seduce her slave [...]". When she heard of their malicious talk, she summoned them and prepared a banquet for them where she gave each a knife and said (to Joseph): "Come out before them". When they saw him, they extolled him, and (in their amazement) cut their hands [...]». The interpretation of the story relates that they were each cutting an orange when Joseph came in and were so overwhelmed by his beauty that, inadvertently, they cut their hands. In this *bayt* the poet takes the situation to extremes by mentioning both hands.

[3] *«We are closer...»* This refers to a qur'ānic verse which states: «[...] and We are closer to him (mankind) than (his) jugular vein.» (Qur'ān, L: 16).

Ghazal XXX.

[1] *Gowhar*, essence, gem. A Persian word, transformed in Arabic into *jowhar*.

Ghazal XXXI.

[1] *Anqā*, or *Sīmurgh*, mythical bird which resides on mount Qāf. He also symbolizes the divine presence, wisdom and Truth.

[2] *Qāf.* See *Ghazal* XVIII[1].

[3] *Kūh-i Sīnā.* See *Ghazal* I[2].

Ghazal XXXII.

[1] *Dalq*, cloak. A metaphor for the human body which has no value compared to the soul and eternal life.

[2] *Āīne-i pur zang*, rusted mirror. Mirror is a metaphor for the human heart, which can be tarnished by worldly attachments. How can a mirror rust? In those days mirrors were made of polished metal, which had to be polished regularly, or they would rust and be unable to offer a reflection.

Ghazal XXXIII.

[1] *Chār mādar* and *haft ābā*, four mothers and seven fathers, refer to the four primary elements and the seven heavens.

Ghazal XXXIV.

[1] *Zohreh*, Venus, symbol of beauty and joy. In Islamic tradition there is a story, mentioned also in the Qur'ān, about two angels, Hārūt and Mārūt, who descend to Earth by order of God to teach humans the art of sorcery. Once on Earth, they become corrupt and fall from grace. Then they are deceived by Zohreh, a woman who obtains from them God's greatest name – which makes anyone possessing it all powerful – and wishes to become a bright star in the heavens.

[2] *Qibla*, that orientation to which Muslims direct their prayers, especially the direction of the *ka'ba*, also of the temple of Jerusalem.

Ghazal XXXV.

[1] *Yā Hū,* one of the most common expressions for remembering God for Muslim mystics and sūfīs. *Yā* is a vocative; *Hū* means «He.»

Ghazal XXXVI.

[1] See *Ghazal* XXIX[2].

Ghazal XXXVIII.

[1] This *bayt* is open to another translation: «But the mirror of the man of [esoteric] knowledge (*ārif*) would not be altered even if I threw all the dust of the world on it.»

Ghazal XXXIX.

[1] *Khatā,* the mediaeval name of northern China (from the name of the Mongol-Turkish people Qara-Hitāy). In Persian poetry, Turk does not necessarily refer to the Turkish people. It indicates the people of the North, with high cheekbones and almond shaped eyes, considered to be the most beautiful people. Also, *Khatā* was a region considered to give rise to the most beautiful women. *Turk-e Khatāī* would possess exceptional beauty.

Ghazal XLI.

[1] *Al mu'min-u mirāt ul mu'min,* is a *hadīth qudsī* (extraqu'rānic revelation of the prophet Muhammad) translated here from Arabic into Persian.

[2] Two of the short *sūra* (CXIII and CXIV) of the last pages of the Qur'ān begin with: «*Qul aūdhu bi rabbel...*», «Say, I seek refuge in God of...». Whereas, *sūra* CXII begins with: «*Qul huwa-llah u ahad...*», «He is God, the one...»

[3] *Hasti.* See *Ghazal* V[5].

Ghazal XLIII.

[1] *Sāqi.* See *Ghazal* I[1].

[2] *Kay Qubād.* The mythical king, founder of the Kiyāni dynasty who, in the Persian epic *Shāh-nāmeh* (The book of the Kings) by Ferdowsi, is said to have lived for one hundred years. *Kay Qubād* is also the middle name of the *saljūq* ruler of Asia Minor, when Rūmī arrived in Konya in 1219 A.D..

Ghazal XLIV.

[1] Refers to verse 53 of *sūra* XX of the Qur'ān: «He who has made for you the earth like a cradle[...]».

[2] *Bād-i Sabā.* See *Ghazal* VII[1].

Ghazal XLV.

[1] *Tiryāq,* theriaca, a composition made up of many ingredients; antidote of every kind against poisons; wine; a sovereign remedy.

[2] *Sormeh* (Arabic, *kuhl*), a black powder/paste, made of various ingredients, used to beautify the eyes and to give better sight. So «collyrium of the soul» would be a remedy for the soul.

Ghazal XLVI.

[1] *Zarr*, used twice here, has two meanings: gold and sun.

[2] *Kahrubā*. See *Ghazal* XI[2].

[3] *Chahār*, four; the four elements. *Panj*, five; might refer to the five senses, the five pillars of the Islamic religion or the five daily prayers. *Shesh*, six; the six directions.

Ghazal XLVII.

[1] *Anqā*. See *Ghazal* XXXI[1].

SELECTED BIBLIOGRAPHY

❖

AHMAD IBN MUḤAMMAD AFLĀKĪ, *Manāqib al-Ārifīn* (ed. Tahsīn Yāzjīī), Türk Tarih Kurumu Basimevi, Ankara 1959-1961, 2 vols. [French trans.: Clement Huart, *Les saints des derviches-tourneurs*, Leroux, Paris 1918-1922].

R. ĀRĀSTEH, *Rūmi the Persian: Rebirth in Creativity and Love*, Ashraf, Lahore 1965.

ARTHUR JOHN ARBERRY, *Classical Persian Literature*, Allen & Unwin, London 1958.

——, *Discourses of Rūmi*, Murray, London 1961. [Annotated translations of the *Fīhi mā Fīhi*].

——, *Mystical Poems of Rūmi*, University of Chicago Press, Chicago 1968, vol. I [First selection: Poems 1-200].

——, *Mystical Poems of Rūmi*, Colo-Westviewer Press, Boulder 1979, vol. II. [Second selection: Poems 201-400].

——, *The Rubā'īyāt of Jalāl al-Din Rūmi*, Walker, London, 1949.

ALESSANDRO BAUSANI, «Djalāl al-Din Rūmi», *Encyclopedia of Islam*, Luzac, London / Leiden 1960, 2nd ed.

PETER J. CHELKOWSKI, *The Scholar and the Saint*, New York University Press, New York 1957.

WILLIAM C. CHITTICK, *The Sufi Path of Love. The Spiritual Teachings of Rūmi*, State University of New York Press, Albany 1983.

MOḤAMMAD ESTE'LĀMĪ, *Masnavī-ye Jalāleddin Mohammad-e Balkhī*, Ketābforūshi-ye Zavvar, Tehran 1982, 6 vols.

BADI'UZAMĀN-I FURŪZĀNFAR, *Ahādīs-e Masnavī*, Tehran University Publications, Tehran 1955.

———, *Risālēh Dar Tahqīq-i Ahwāl wa Zindigānī-ye Mawlānā Jalāl al-dīn Mohammad*, Tehran 1954, 2nd ed.

———, *Kullīyāt-e Shams*, Tehran University Publications, Tehran 1957-1968.

———, *Sharh-i Mathnawi*, Tehran University Publications, Tehran 1967-1969, 3 vols. [incomplete].

SĀDEQ GOWHARĪN, *Farhang-e Loqāt va ta'bīrāt-e Mathnavī*, Tehran University Publications, Tehran, 1959-1960, 5 vols. [incomplete].

JALĀL HUMĀ'Ī, *Mawlavī-nāmeh, yā Mowlavī cheh mīgūyad*, Showrā-ye Ālī-ye Farhang o Honar, Tehran 1965-1966, 2 vols.

MOḤAMMAD 'ALĪ MOVAHED, *Khomi az Sharūb-e Rabbānī, Gozīdeh-ye Maqālāt-e Shams*, Enteshārāt-e Sokhan, Tehran 1994.

———, *Ostorlāb-e Haq, Gozīdeh-ye Fihi mā Fihi*, Enteshārāt-e Sokhan, Tehran 1992.

REYNOLD ALLEYNE NICHOLSON, *Selected Poems from the Dīvāni Shamsi Tabrīz*, Cambridge, 1898.

———, *The Mathnawī of Jalālu'ddin Rūmi*, Luzac, London 1925-1940, 8 vols.

———, *Rūmi, Poet and Mystic*, Allen & Unwin, London 1950.

MOḤAMMAD-REZA SHAFI'Ī-YE KADKANI, *Gozīdeh-ye Ghazaliyāt-e Shams*, Shereckat-e Sahāmi-ye Ketābhā-ye Jībi, Tehran 1999, 12th ed.

NĀSERADDĪN SĀHEBAZZAMĀNĪ, *Khatt-e Sevvom*, Atāī Publications, Tehran 1973.

ANNEMARIE SCHIMMEL, *The Triumphal Sun*, East-West Publications, London 1978.

——, *I am Wind, You are Fire*, Shambala, Boston / London 1992.
——, *As Through a Veil: Mystical Poetry in Islam*, Columbia University Press, New York 1982.

'ABDOLHOSSEIN ZARRĪNKŪB, *Pelleh Pelleh tā Molāqāt-e Khodā: on the Life and Thoughts of Rūmi*, Entesharat-e Elmi, Tehran 1994.

Mirror Basmalah,
Turkey, nineteenth century.

BIOGRAPHICAL NOTE

✣

MUḤAMMAD JALĀL AD-DĪN BALKHI, KNOWN AS RŪMĪ IN THE WESTERN WORLD, was born in Balkh, a major city of greater Khurasān, in today's Afghanistan. His date of birth is recorded as the year 1207 A.D.

His father, Bahā' ad-dīn Walad, a prominent theologian of the time, had many students and followers. According to some scholars, his power frightened the Prince of Balkh, 'Alā ad-dīn Khwārazm Shāh, who was famous for his rivalries with the Caliph of Baghdād. A few years after the birth of Jalāl ad-dīn, his father left his homeland, accompanied by all the members of his family and a large number of followers. The cause of this migration could have been his falling out of grace with the Prince, the imminent Mongol invasion of the region, or both. In any case, he travelled toward the West and stayed in Nishapūr for some time.

According to tradition, Bahā' ad-dīn was a friend of the well known mystic poet Farīd ad-dīn 'Aṭṭār, who predicted a great spiritual future for the young Jalāl ad-dīn. Continuing the migration towards the Western regions, Bahā' ad-dīn and his entourage, after having made the pilgrimage to Mecca, finally arrived in Asia Minor and settled in Konya, the capital of the Seljuq Kingdom, where they were received with respect by the ruler, 'Alā ad-dīn Kay Qubād.

Ten years later Bahā' ad-dīn died and Jalāl ad-dīn continued to teach and preach in the manner of his father until the arrival in Konya of Shams-i Tabrīz, who would become his spiritual teacher. Shams caused a radical transformation in his life; he stopped preaching orthodox Islamic theology. That is when he became a poet and uttered thousands of ecstatic verses, making an enormous contribution to the already rich mysitcal literature of Persia.

Rumi's major works are: the *Dīvān-i Shams-i Tabrīz*, in ten volumes; the *Masnavī [Masnavī-e Ma'navī]*, written in the latter part of his life, which consist of more than 26,000 verses; and the *Fīhi mā fīhi [There Is What There Is] (Discourses)*. These works have been translated into English, with commentary, by Reynold A. Nicholson and by A.J. Arberry.

Rumi died in 1273 A.D.
He is buried in Konya.

❀

GLOSSARY

❧

'Aql	Intellect.
Awliyā'	Saints, friends of God.
— *mastur*	Hidden.
Bayt	Couplet.
Daf	A percussion instrument; a handheld drum made of a wooden ring and sheepskin, similar to the Irish or the American Indian drum.
Dars	Lesson, study.
Fatwā	Religious decree issued by a high Islamic clergy.
Fanā'	Annihilation. *Cfr.* Qur'ān LV: 26: «All that is on earth will perish *[fān]*: but will abide (for ever) the Face of thy Lord, full of Majesty, Bounty and Honour.» The ultimate goal of a mystic is to become annihilated in God, therefore returning to the source. The metaphor for such a transformation, employed frequently in Persian poetry, is a moth being burned by a candle flame, thus becoming one with it. According to sūfī technical terminology, *fanā* is one of the spiritual 'stations' (*maqām*, pl. *maqāmāt*) of the soul.
Faqīh	Isalamic theologian and jurisprudent.
Fiqh	Islamic jurisprudence.

Ghazal	Form of Persian lyrical poem of usually seven to twelve lines in which the first hemistich of the first couplet and all second hemistiches rhyme.
Ḥadīth	Tradition. Saying of the prophet Muhammad tranmistted by a chain of known intermediaries.
— *qudsī*	Extraqur'ānic revelation.
Hajj	One of the duties of every Muslim is to travel to Mecca for pilgrimage at least once in his or her lifetime, if finances allow it. The proper time for the pilgrimage is in the month of *dhul-hajja* of the Muslim calendar.
Irshad	Guidance.
'Ishq	Love. According to sūfī technical terminology, one of the spiritual 'states' (*ḥāl*, pl. *ahwāl*) of the soul.
Ka'ba	Any square building; the sanctuary of Mecca. All Muslims face the Ka'ba for prayer.
Khaniqāh	Place of gathering for sūfīs.
Madrisa	Theological school.
Maktab	Children's school.
Majles	Gathering.
— *dars*	See *dars*.
Maqalat	Discourses.
Mi'raj	A flight of steps, ladder, ascent. The journey of the prophet Muhammad to heaven to meet with God.
Misra'	Hemistich.
Mowlānā	Honorific title, meaning «Our lord». In Persian, Rūmī is commonly called *Mowlānā* and in Turkish *Mevlānā*.
Murid	Adept, desciple.
Nay	A flute made of a simple piece of reed with holes, about two feet long. It emits a soft and melodic sound.
Pīr	Elder, a spiritual teacher.

DĪVĀN-I SHAMS-I TABRĪZ ♦ GLOSSARY

Qāf Mythical mountain which surrounds the world and has mystical properties.

Qibla The direction to which Muslims direct their prayers, principally toward the *ka'ba*, and also toward the Temple of Jerusalem.

Samā' Literally «to listen.» In sūfī tradition *samā'* means to perform ecstatic dance by listening to spiritual music.

Sāqi Cupbearer. Usually a beautiful young man, who would make the rounds in a tavern with a cup of wine and placate the drinkers. *Sāqi* is used profusely in Persian mystical poetry and often represents the beloved, a spiritual teacher or even the face of God.

Sheikh Religious or spiritual leader. In sūfī terminology *sheikh* is a rank which is below the *pīr* and is, usually, appointed by the *pīr*.

Sultān King.

'Ulamā Scientists, theologians. Plural of *'alim*.

Tarīqa Literally, path, which indicates a sūfī order.

Walāyat Derived from *walī*. An exalted spiritual status. According to sūfī doctrine, a *walī* is a friend of God and his/her will is the will of God.

Yā Hū One of the most common expressions for remembering God for Muslim mystics and sūfīs. *Yā* is a vocative; *Hū* means «He.»

Zulfaqār The famous sword of 'Alī. The followers of 'Alī believe that the souls of the unbelievers, who died by his sword in the holy wars, were saved and went to paradise.

» VISIONI «

ENRICO ALLIATA, *Spregiudicanda. Pensieri e aforismi.*

MIGUEL ÁNGEL ASTURIAS, *Leggende del Guatemala.* Prologo di Paul Valéry.

MIRKO BEVILACQUA, *Il giardino del piacere. Saggi sul Decameron.* PREMIO GRINZANE CAVOUR - HANBURY 1996. (2° ED.).

SYLVANO BUSSOTTI, *Lettura del Tieste*, Prefazione di Giovanna Morelli Luporini.

RENZO CIGOI, *Quattrocento domande a un vecchio ebreo triestino. Colloqui con Giorgio Voghera.*

AMALIA DEL PONTE, *La forma del suono.*

YŪNUS EMRE, *Dīvān.* Cura, introduzione e traduzione e note di Anna Masala.

FEDERICO FELLINI, *Imago. Appunti di un visionario.* Introduzione di Toni Maraini. (2ª ED.).

FEDERICO GARCÍA LORCA, *Il duende. Teoria e giuoco.* Testo originale a fronte. Introduzioni di Elémire Zolla, Valentí Gómez i Oliver e José F.A. Oliver.(2° ED.).

JOHANN WOLFGANG VON GOETHE, *Il trionfo del sentimentalismo.* Versione di Ettore Brissa. A cura, e con introduzione, di Massimo Venturi Ferriolo.

JOHANN WOLFGANG VON GOETHE, *I Segreti e la Massoneria.* Introduzione, versione e cura di Ettore Brissa. Prefazione di Marino Freschi.

HANS KAISER, *Akróasis. La teoria dell'armonia del mondo.* Prefazione dell'Autore, postfazione di Julius Schwabe. (2ª ED.).

MARIO LUZI, *Il colore della poesia.* A cura di Doriano Fasoli. Introduzione di Maria Luisa Spaziani.

FOSCO MARAINI, *Il nuvolario. Principî di nubignosia.* Introduzione di Toni Maraini. (3° ED.).

SHAMS NADIR, *L'astrolabio del mare.* Prefazione di Jorge Amado, introduzione di Leopold S. Senghor.

DIONYSUS PETAVIUS, *Antico calendario romano.* Introduzione e note di Massimiliano Kornmüller.

JALĀL AD-DĪN RŪMĪ, *Dīvān-i Shams-i Tabrīz.* Testo persiano originale a fronte. Cura, traduzione e note di Iraj Anvar; prefazione di Peter Chelkowski; Introduzione di Moḥammad 'Alī Movahed. Con CD.

» VISIONI « IMMINENTI

NASSREDDĪN KHOGIA, *Astuzie & Facezie. Il sorriso di un maestro.* Intraduzione, traduzione e note di Anna Masala

ATTILIO BERTOLUCCI, *La grazia di un pensiero.* A cura di Doriano Fasoli.

*This book has been set in ten, nine and eight
point Monotype Garamond one point leaded,
according to the Publisher's layout
and printed in March 2002 by
Tipografia della Pace,
in Rome, Italy.*

❦

We are delighted to offer a CD with Iraj Anvar reading twenty-eight Ghazals of this collection so that our readers may appreciate the lyrics of the original Persian.

SEMAR PUBLISHERS

❦

When Iraj asked me if I would write some comments for his reading of Rumi I was flattered. I have always considered Rūmī's voice the most beautiful in expressing the ordeal of mystics. Since I do not know Persian, all my knowledge of Rūmī comes from French, English and Turkish. By knowing the quality of Persian from hearing Iraj speak, I was thrilled when I heard he was recording Rūmī in his native tongue. Many people speak of Rūmī as one of the greatest mystics of Isalm. To my way of thinking, it is impossible to classify mystics as Islamic, Christian, Jewish, Hindu, Buddhist, or any other religion. There is only one sort of mystic, no matter how attained. A mystic is a human who has become ONE *with God.*

If it is possible to have many kinds of Gods, it follows there could be many kinds of mystics. Furthermore, it cannot be imagined there being a better or lesser mystic: a human can be a mystic or not a mystic. Mystic is a word expressing the superlative as it is, such as the single word PERFECT. *There cannot be more perfect or less perfect, perfecter, perfectest. There is only one single indication of a true mystic: vibrating always in the altruistic body energy of Consciousness. And Mowlana Jalāl-ad-dīn Rūmī is the first human who established and put into practice the concept of lending a helpful hand to others, instead of becoming a recluse in a cave after experiencing communion with the Eternal Spirit of Creative and Sustaining Power.*

I hope you enjoy his work (may God bless his attainment).

MURAT YAGAN
Kebzeh Foundation

❦

THE PRODUCTION OF THIS CD WAS MADE POSSIBLE BY A GENEROUS CONTRIBUTION
FROM THE KEBZEH FOUNDATION, VERNON, B.C., CANADA.

℗ SOUND ENGINEER: RON LLEAR